Behind History

DISCOVERY BOOKS

BEHIND HISTORY

Ray C. Stedman

Word Books, Publisher
Waco, Texas

Discovery Books are published by Word Books,
Publishers in cooperation with Discovery Foundation, Palo Alto, California.

Library of Congress catalog card number: 75–36181

Printed in the United States of America

Titles by Ray C. Stedman in
the Discovery Books series . . .

Authentic Christianity

Jesus Teaches on Prayer

Spiritual Warfare

Understanding Man

Behind History

Death of a Nation

Contents

1

The Mystery of History

Within two years of the close of the Book of Acts, a great fire broke out in Rome for which the Christians were blamed, bringing on the first widespread persecution of Christians by the Roman empire. And within eight years came that terrible, troublous time in Palestine when the Jews rebelled against the authority of Rome and a Roman army under Titus subjected Jerusalem to probably the most dreadful siege in all history. Thousands and thousands of Jews died within the city, with many starving to death in a great famine caused by the siege. Eventually the city was captured as Jesus had predicted it would be. The temple was invaded and burned to the ground, with every stone overturned so that "not one stone was left standing upon another." If you visit Rome today, you can still see the great Arch of Titus, erected in commemoration of that conquest.

Most people are of the opinion that the close of Acts is the end of the inspired record of church history and that in the Bible we have no hint of the developments that were to arise in history after the events recorded in Acts. But we are not left without help in this area. Many Bible scholars find that there are several major passages of Scripture which deal in a sweeping, broad way with what was to follow in human history after Acts.

One of these passages is in the opening chapters of the Book of Revelation, where we have the letters to the seven churches of Asia from the hand of John, written as he received them in a vision of Jesus Christ. Although these letters were written to actual churches which existed in the Roman empire at that time, nevertheless, many feel, and I agree, that these are also predictive of certain stages through which the church would pass. As history has unfolded itself, we have found that those letters have indeed accurately predicted what has happened within the church throughout the ages that have followed.

Two other well-known passages of this nature occur in Matthew. One of these, with corresponding passages in Mark and Luke, is the "Olivet Discourse," the sermon delivered by Jesus on the Mount of Olives just before his crucifixion. As he sat there with his disciples and looked out over the city of Jerusalem, he knew that his death was near. And in the most amazing terms he described what would happen in the centuries that followed, when nation would rise against nation, and wars, famines, and earthquakes would characterize the whole period. Eventually, he said, a world government would develop, headed by a great leader who would exalt himself as God and the world would follow after him. Then God would bring about a time of great trouble such as the world had never seen from its beginning till its end. At the end of that time Jesus would appear again for all the earth to see and establish his kingdom. You can find that well-known passage in Matthew 24 and 25.

But I want to turn now to the other passage which occurs earlier in the Gospel of Matthew. We might call it the "Sermon by the Sea." Jesus gave three great messages which are recorded in Matthew: the Sermon on the Mount (chapters 5 through 7); the Sermon by the Sea (chapter 13), and the Olivet Discourse (chapters 24 and 25). The passage in Matthew 13, less well known than the Olivet Discourse, consists of seven parables which our Lord told all in one day. In them he traces not the *events* of history but the *principles* which affect all of human life during what we call the present age, the age between his comings.

I propose that we study these great parables very carefully, relating them to their corresponding fulfillments in history. We are going to look at history in the light of what Jesus has revealed will be the governing factors of human life during this period. We will see history, therefore, as God sees it. All of us are familiar

with history as man sees it—the rather meaningless
jumble of kings and empires, presidents and wars, discoveries, betrayals and exploitations, which constitute
what we call the record of history. That is at best a
very twisted and distorted view. But in these seven
parables we want to look behind the scenes of history,
through the eyes of Jesus Christ, at the forces which
are at work in human lives to *bring about* the events
that are recorded in our newspapers and history
books. This is God's view of history.

   This series of parables began on a very eventful day
when Jesus had been teaching in the synagogue at
Capernaum. Matthew tells us,

> That same day Jesus went out of the house and sat be-
> side the sea. And great crowds gathered about him, so
> that he got into a boat and sat there; and the whole
> crowd stood on the beach. And he told them many
> things in parables . . . (Matt. 13:1–3).

Notice the very beautiful natural setting that Matthew
records for us. It is on the northern shore of the Sea
of Galilee, not very far from the scene of our Lord's
first great message, the Sermon on the Mount. Jesus
has come out of the synagogue at Capernaum and
gone down to the beach, and *great* crowds have
gathered—Matthew does not tell us how many people,
but it must have been well into the thousands. They
are drawn by the power that our Lord has displayed
and by the wisdom of his words, and they are ready
to see and hear more. In order to be able to address
them he pushes out from shore in a boat and there he
begins to teach this great crowd of people.

A MOST UNUSUAL DAY

Before we come to the parables themselves, I want
to take time to look at the context of this most remarkable day in our Lord's life. There is a puzzling
new development here in the ministry and teaching of
Jesus which we ought to note. To understand it fully,
we need to go back to chapter 12, where the record
of this day begins. Jesus was teaching in the synagogue, and he began by quoting a most unusual passage from Isaiah, a prophecy that the message of God
would go out to the Gentiles. Throughout the early
part of our Lord's ministry, he emphasized that he had
come to the lost sheep of the house of Israel. He sel-
dom said anything about the Gentiles, but now he
quotes this passage from Isaiah:

> Behold, my servant whom I have chosen,
>   my beloved with whom my soul is well pleased.
> I will put my Spirit upon him,
>   and he shall proclaim justice to the Gentiles.
> He will not wrangle or cry aloud,
>   nor will any one hear his voice in the streets;
> he will not break a bruised reed
>   or quench a smoldering wick,
> till he brings justice to victory;
>   and in his name will the Gentiles hope
>   (Matt. 12:18–21).

And on that strange note he went on to say some very
solemn words to Israel. He warned them about the
possibility of committing the unpardonable sin of
blasphemy against the Holy Spirit (vs. 32). He said
to them, "Either make the tree good, and its fruit

good; or make the tree bad, and its fruit bad; for the tree is known by its fruit" (vs. 33). That is, "Come out into the open and stop being hypocritical!" And then, in response to the Pharisees' insistence on a sign, Jesus announced to this great crowd of Jews in the synagogue,

> . . . no sign shall be given . . . except the sign of the prophet Jonah. For as Jonah was three days and three nights in the belly of the whale, so will the Son of man be three days and three nights in the heart of the earth (vss. 39–40).

In other words, the resurrection is to be the sign to Israel that God is behind the whole enterprise of sending Jesus and that he is indeed their promised Messiah. Then he went on to warn them about the danger of being reinhabited by demons after they had once been cleansed. Finally, at the close of chapter 12, he spoke of the priority of spiritual relationships over natural ones:

> While he was still speaking to the people, behold, his mother and his brothers stood outside, asking to speak to him. But he replied to the man who told him, "Who is my mother, and who are my brothers?" And stretching out his hand toward his disciples, he said, "Here are my mother and my brothers! For whoever does the will of my Father in heaven is my brother, and sister, and mother" (Matt. 12:46–50).

And having said those unusual words, Jesus went out that same day and sat beside the sea and began to teach the crowds these parables. That bit of background is necessary in order to understand that something strange is happening here in these parables. A

corner has been turned. Jesus is unfolding truth that
he has never revealed before. Furthermore, he begins
to employ a new method of teaching, one that he hasn't
used before. As far as we can tell by comparing the
record of the Gospels, this is the first time that Jesus
ever spoke in parables. It is true that he often employed metaphors and similes, and he was constantly
referring to pictures drawn from life around him. But
this is the first time that he ever spoke in stories containing a hidden spiritual message. So the disciples are
struck by this, and Matthew records their reaction:

> Then the disciples came and said to him, "Why do you
> speak to them in parables?" And he answered them,
> "To you it has been given to know the secrets of the
> kingdom of heaven, but to them it has not been given.
> For to him who has will more be given, and he will have
> abundance; but from him who has not, even what he has
> will be taken away. This is why I speak to them in par-
> ables, because seeing they do not see, and hearing they
> do not hear, nor do they understand. With them indeed
> is fulfilled the prophecy of Isaiah which says:
> 'You shall indeed hear but never understand,
>   and you shall indeed see but never perceive.
> For this people's heart has grown dull,
>   and their ears are heavy of hearing,
>   and their eyes they have closed.
> lest they should perceive with their eyes,
>   and hear with their ears,
> and understand with their heart,
>   and turn for me to heal them.'
> But blessed are your eyes, for they see, and your ears,
> for they hear. Truly, I say to you, many prophets and
> righteous men longed to see what you see, and did not
> see it, and to hear what you hear, and did not hear it"
> (Matt. 13:10–17).

That is undoubtedly one of the most important and revealing paragraphs in the whole Bible. It contains what might well be called "the key to history," the great principle upon which God acts to determine human events. What Jesus is setting before us in this series of parables is all based upon the great principle which he declares in the midst of this paragraph. You will never understand what is happening in current events nor in the whole scope of history unless you understand this principle. It is not only the principle by which God judges nations and determines the course of international events but it is also the principle by which he governs what happens to individuals.

So before we study the parables we want to look at this interlude in which Jesus answers his disciples' question. I want to examine four things with you in this section. First, we want to look more closely at the question the disciples asked, and at our Lord's answer to them. Next, I want to pull out this central principle on which all of history turns. We will see, thirdly, how this principle is illustrated by the nation Israel, and finally, we want to understand the unique privilege enjoyed by these disciples which we now share in hearing these things. Now, look once more at the question with me:

Then the disciples came and said to him, "Why do you speak to them in parables?" And he answered them, "To you it has been given to know the secrets of the kingdom of heaven, but to them it has not been given" (vss. 10–11).

I am sure that it was curiosity which prompted these disciples to question Jesus. They had never heard our Lord talk this way before, and they could not understand it. It is clear that they did not understand the meaning of the stories, since Jesus had to explain some of them. And neither did they understand why he used this approach. So, puzzled and curious, they came to him and said, "Why are you doing this?"

SHARING SECRETS

His answer must have pleased them greatly, because he said, "Well, to *you* it has been given to know the secrets of the kingdom of heaven, but to them it has not been given." The word translated "secrets" means, literally, "mysteries." In Scripture a mystery is a truth which cannot be known by the normal exercise of human wisdom and knowledge. It is a truth concerning life which God must tell us about if we are to know it, because it could never be discovered by the exercise of human intelligence. That is why these secrets, these mysteries about the kingdom of heaven, and therefore about life, will never be found in science or literature or history or any other discipline of human knowledge or investigation. They are simply not there, and yet they are essential to the understanding of life. But they must be disclosed to us by God.

This is why man's wisdom is never enough. We can discover many things about life, and we can invent a lot of useful implements and gadgets. But we will never, never explain or fulfill human life on those terms. We must know more, and only God can tell us. That is why these mysteries are of great importance.

The gospel itself is one of these mysteries. Its great secret, Paul says, is "Christ in you, the hope of glory." And Paul announced in several of his letters that it was given to the apostles to unfold these great mysteries of the kingdom of heaven. But the unfolding began with Jesus.

These disciples must have been pleased as punch when Jesus said to them, "To you it has been given to know, but not to them." That made them feel like a special "in" group, the privileged few. That is a great feeling, isn't it? We all like that wonderful feeling when somebody gathers us in close and says, "Come here, I want to tell you something. Don't tell anyone else; this is only for you." What a delicious morsel to chew on! We are instantly all ears. It only confirms what we have suspected about ourselves all along—that we are superior people with a special ability which others do not have, therefore, we have a right to know things which are hidden from others.

You can imagine the pride these disciples must have felt. But our Lord pricks that balloon of pride instantly. He goes on to tell them the basis upon which they were chosen and not someone else; it is simply this: "For to him who has will more be given, and he will have abundance; but from him who has not, even what he has will be taken away" (vs. 12). That is a basic, fundamental law of life. It is the great principle upon which God operates to govern human lives and human history. "To him who has will more be given . . . but from him who has not, even what he has [or as Luke says, 'even what he thinks he has'] will be taken away." Now, what does that mean? It is so fundamental that it applies to everything in life, to every realm of existence. It is even true on the physical level. Suppose you deliberately refuse to use one of the muscles of your body? You will find that soon it will begin to weaken and atrophy, and that what you have is taken away. All you need to do to render your arm useless is to simply tie it up and not use it for a few months. Soon you will find you have lost the ability to use it. All of life operates on this principle.

REJECTED TRUTH IS LOST

Reduced to its simplest terms, the principle means this: Truth must be acted upon in order to be retained. Truth rejected or unused is lost. God is constantly confronting men with truth about everything at every level of life. Man is so constructed that he is made to act upon truth. But if he doesn't, he loses the truth which has already been given to him. That is a very vital and important principle in understanding human life. It is the basis upon which God determines advance or regression either in individuals or in nations.

This fantastically important statement explains, for example, why the disciples were called. When the Lord saw them—simple fishermen, tax collectors, ordinary men—he saw in the heart of each one a willingness to act on truth. When they saw the truth and knew it to be truth, they acted on it. The proof of that is the way they responded when he called them. The moment he said to them, "Come, follow me," they rose and followed him. They acted on truth, and Jesus had perceived that in them. That is why it was given to them to know the secrets while to others it was hidden. Their willingness to act on the truth they knew qualified them for more truth.

I once heard about a young man whose sweater a friend admired. The young man had recently become a Christian. He was reading Scripture daily and growing in the Lord. When his friend complimented him on his sweater, the young man paused a moment, took his sweater off and handed it to his friend, and said, "Here, you take it." Astonished, the friend asked him why he was giving his sweater away. He replied, "Because I've been reading the Bible and I learned there that Christians are to be generous with their possessions. So I want to start practicing that, and I want you to have this sweater."

Since I heard about that, I've been admiring quite a few things, but I must say that the degree of obedience to this truth has been discouragingly slight! But that is a beautiful illustration of just exactly what Jesus meant—a willingness to act on truth, not to say that it applies to someone else—not to procrastinate, but to begin immediately to act upon it, to risk, to lose, if necessary, in order to step out on truth that is learned. That, he says, is the secret of advance and growth in Christian life.

One of the wonderfully encouraging aspects of life today is the tremendous spiritual growth we are seeing in young people who are coming to Christ out of the despair and emptiness of existential rationalism. These young men and women are hearing truth, and when they hear it, they act on it. That is why some of them are advancing to maturity with such leaps and bounds that they are putting to shame many who have been Christians for years. They are ready to act on what they know. That explains their rapid progress in the gospel.

The truths to which they are responding have been there in the Scriptures for centuries. They have been taught in churches in every section of the land. But for some reason, very few seem to want to take them seriously, to obey them. If any church or individual would experience the blessing of God, they must become simple enough to believe and obey what God has said. Try it, and you will find immediately that to those who have, more will be given, and they shall have in abundance.

FALLEN EMPIRES

But the contrary is also true. If you don't obey truth, it is taken away from you. This great principle is visible in international affairs. Why, for instance, has Great Britain lost its empire and been reduced to a second-rate power after being the leading nation of the world for so many decades? The answer is that the English people knew truth which they failed to act on. They did not incorporate into their economic and national life the truth which they admitted widely as a people. They were false to principles they knew to be true, and as a result, their scepter of power has been removed and they have sunk into relative obscurity. There is no other explanation for it. You can talk about economics, about politics, and other such things, but those are merely the processes by which this principle is worked out.

Why did the Roman empire fall before the barbarian hordes after it had been queen of the world for centuries? The answer is that when its paganism was confronted with the truth of the cross of Christ, it rejected that truth and fought back with fire and sword and wild beasts and cruel tortures. And the empire crumbled from within. All the wisdom of the Roman senate and all the experience garnered in centuries of world dominion were unable to hold that empire together.

Why are the Russian people now deprived of the right to worship, of freedom of speech and of the press, and forbidden to travel abroad or even to read of other cultures? Because when the truth of the gospel was widespread in Russia, as once it was, it was canonized and ritualized and emptied of its content until it became a hollow shell of pretense and religious hypocrisy. When that happened, the nation was rendered ripe for revolution.

What do you think is happening in the United States today? This nation is facing exactly that same possibility. The open rejection of the truth about Jesus Christ on the part of the American people, truth which they have known and seen, and the hollow pretense of obeying it when they really do not believe it, is dimming the light in this land and removing the barriers to savagery and violence . . . and the barbarians are at the doors again. And evangelicals can be as guilty as anyone else in this respect.

This, then, is the great principle upon which God determines history. It is illustrated in Israel, as Jesus goes on to show: "This is why I speak to them in parables, because seeing they do not see, and hearing they do not hear, nor do they understand" (vs. 13).

And then he quotes Isaiah, saying that 725 years previously Isaiah had predicted that this would be the case—that when this people heard and saw the truth, they would not understand it nor receive it: "With them indeed is fulfilled the prophecy of Isaiah which says: 'You shall indeed hear but never understand, and you shall indeed see but never perceive'" (vs. 14).

What does Jesus mean? Well, the fact that he spoke in parables was the beginning of the process of taking away the truth from a people who would not receive it. They had it, but they did not act on it. Jesus spoke very plainly to them at the beginning. They knew he spoke the truth—they even said so: "Never man spake like this man. Where has this man received this wisdom? Why is it that he teaches us not as the scribes and Pharisees but with authority?" They watched him and listened to his matchless words. Crowds were greatly attracted to him and followed wherever he went. But only a relative handful did anything about it.

VEILED TRUTH

And so the time came when he began to veil the truth. That is what a parable is—a veiled, hidden truth. It is truth being removed, taken away. Jesus says, "This is why I am speaking to them in parables—because they will not see. They have the truth set before them and they will not act. They will not understand, just as Isaiah said." Then he quotes Isaiah further: " 'For this people's heart has grown dull, and their ears are heavy of hearing, and their eyes they have closed . . .' "

Do you notice who did this? It does not say that God dulled this people's heart and stopped their ears and closed their eyes. *They* did it. *Their* eyes *they* closed, *their* heart *they* have made to grow dull, *their* ears *they* have stopped up. Why? Well, as Isaiah said, " '. . . lest they should perceive with their eyes, and hear with their ears, and understand with their heart, and turn for me to heal them' " (vs. 15).

In other words, they understood what he was after, and they sensed deep inside that he could do what he said he would do. He could heal this nation, heal its hurt, its sickness and weakness, its darkness and slavery. But the amazing thing is that these people did not want what God wanted to give them. They didn't want to be healed. They sensed that in the coming of Jesus, God was reaching out to them to restore them, to make them whole. And in the terrible perversity of their hearts they didn't want it. They preferred their own evil, weakness, and folly because to be healed meant to confess and to acknowledge that they were wrong. Their pride had to be humbled, and they weren't ready to pay that price. This is the terrible judgment that our Lord brings down upon history. He said, "Light has come into the world and men love darkness rather than light. That is the condemnation.

"And because of that," he says, "I am going to speak to them in parables. I will still tell them the truth, because I am truth. I cannot speak anything else but truth. But they will not hear it nor understand it. Only those who are prepared to act upon what they hear will understand it." That is the great lesson which forms the background of these parables.

TWICE BLESSED

But then in contrast Jesus said to his disciples, "How happy you are, how privileged you are!" "Blessed are your eyes, for they see, and your ears, for they hear" (vs. 16). That is, "You are ready to act, and thank God for that. And what a blessing this will bring to you, because you can get more truth!" They were twice blessed, he said, because: "Truly, I say to you, many prophets and righteous men longed to see what you see, and did not see it, and to hear what you hear, and did not hear it" (vs. 17).

Here he is thinking back across the whole range of the Old Testament, thinking of Isaiah and Jeremiah and Daniel, Elijah and Elisha and Samuel, of David and Moses, and all the others. He is saying that the Spirit of God, speaking through them, showed them there would be a revelation of truth the like of which man had never seen before. It would be in the coming of a person who would speak and perform the ultimate unfolding of truth. Nothing that the mind of man in its present capacity could ever grasp would be omitted in that unfolding. And he says, "You are those people. How happy you are! How carefully you ought to listen to this because this is the final, ultimate revelation of truth the way God sees it, the hidden answer to all the problems and confusion of life. You are so fortunate because you are seeing what men have longed to see for centuries."

We stand with those disciples today. These words are addressed to us because we can see what they saw. We can hear what they heard, and, like them, we are truly blessed. We have set before us the unfolding of the secrets of life. If we don't hear it, if we don't grasp it, if we don't heed it, we have only ourselves to blame. God has given to us not only the life that comes from Jesus Christ but also the promise that he will unfold to us all the understanding we need to meet any difficult problem or circumstance of life and to see it as God sees it—if we but give ourselves to the study and understanding of his Word. As Paul says, "In Christ are hidden all the treasures of wisdom and knowledge" (Col. 2:3).

PREPARE TO ACT

As you look around at life today, it is very obvious that something is terribly lacking in the understanding of men. We have vast technological ability and can construct all kinds of useful machines and improve the physical standard of our lives, but something is still missing. We do not know how to enable people to live in harmony with one another. We do not know how to remove the frictions, the hostilities, the guilt of man. We do not know how to heal his hurt. And yet those secrets are given to us, but only to those prepared to act upon them. That is the key.

This is why it is so terribly important that when God teaches you something, you do not delay acting on it. Do not just put it up on your wall and say, "I learned a great truth today. It blessed my heart. There it is; you can read it for yourself." No, act on it!

This means that when you read in the Scriptures that Christians are to practice hospitality without grudging, you should go home, open your door, and invite somebody in—use your home without grudging, without partiality, for the benefit of those who are in need. This means that when the Lord, through Paul, says, "Be kind to one another, tenderhearted, forgiving one another, as God in Christ forgave you," if you have a grudge in your heart against somebody—you are resentful and have been trying to hurt them, or you have excluded them or turned your back on them —then go and deal with that situation, heal that relationship. Act upon the truth. If you don't, you are committing yourself to blindness, and you will find that the truth which would have delivered you will be taken away. All you will have left is a hollow shell of words, with no content whatever.

Our Lord is putting his finger right on the great mystery of history, the secret of human life. How des-

perately we need to understand this and to follow it.
As we go into this passage in succeeding chapters, we
will study these mysteries, these parables one by one.
And each will unveil something to us. May God grant
that our hearts will be prepared to listen *and to act,*
because it is as we act, that new truth is given and we
begin to unfold like a flower before the rising sun as
God causes our life to blossom with an abundance of
fruit and knowledge.

> Our Lord Jesus, we wait before you, awed and
> humbled by these words. We know that in you
> are hidden great and marvelous truths which
> man has never grasped and which we desperately
> need to know. Our happiness depends upon it.
> We pray that you will make us willing to act
> upon what you do show us. Save us from the folly
> of sitting back in scornful scepticism, waiting to
> have everything unveiled to us before we will
> act on it. Help us to act upon those bits and
> pieces of truth which come to us, Lord, and
> which we know are true. For then, according to
> your promise: "To him who has will more be
> given, and he will have abundance." And help us
> to take seriously this warning: "But from him
> who has not, even what he has will be taken
> away." We ask it in your name, Amen.

2

The Case
of the Lavish Farmer

The parables, Jesus said, are hidden to those who do not pay attention, who do not listen, but are open to those who do. His constant warning throughout is, "He who has ears to hear, let him hear." So we are invited to give close attention to these parables through which we can understand the times in which we live.

Like a mystery novel, each parable contains certain clues that are given to guide us to its meaning. Our Lord began by interpreting the first two parables for the disciples, thus giving them the pattern of interpretation—the process to follow in discovering what the other parables mean. Then he left them on their own, as he does us, with a little additional help on the last parable. Therefore, each of these parables challenges us to think through what our Lord means by it and each contains a great revelation which is essential for us to understand. So as we go through them, I hope the desire will grow in you to pick up all the clues that God has given and to understand what he is saying in these unusual stories about the secrets of the kingdom of heaven.

HERE, THERE, EVERYWHERE

The first story is about a farmer who broadcasts his seed with a lavish hand, flinging it about with no concern for where it falls:

> And he told them many things in parables, saying, "A sower went out to sow. And as he sowed, some seeds fell along the path, and the birds came and devoured them. Other seeds fell on rocky ground, where they had not much soil, and immediately they sprang up, since they had no depth of soil, but when the sun rose they were scorched; and since they had no root they withered away. Other seeds fell upon thorns, and the thorns grew up and choked them. Other seeds fell on good soil and brought forth grain, some a hundredfold, some sixty, some thirty. He who has ears, let him hear" (Matt. 13:3–9).

It is very likely that when our Lord was telling this story, the whole scene was being enacted right before the eyes of these people. This was springtime, and from where they stood on the beach, they could probably look up on the hillside and see a sower going forth to sow. They could see a path which had been beaten across the field and the birds picking up the seeds right behind the sower. They could see the rocky ground, and the thorns and thistles growing up, and the good soil of the field. This was the way Jesus taught. He often picked up something that was happening right around his hearers and used it as an illustration of the great truth he wanted to convey.

But when he finished, there must have been many puzzled looks on the faces of people in this crowd. They were waiting, of course, for an explanation. He told a story; it was being enacted right in front of them—but what did it mean? It was at this point, Matthew tells us, that the disciples came to him. Evidently the people waited and waited, and the pause became so embarrassing that the disciples finally came and said to him, "Why do you speak to them in parables?"

Our Lord's explanation, which we have already examined, is that God is operating on the fundamental principle that to him who has, more will be given; but from him who has not, even what he has will be taken away. That seems most unfair, doesn't it? But we must understand that when the Lord says, "To him who has," he is speaking about the possession of truth—truth which is acted on. You never have truth when you merely have it in your head. You have truth only when you have acted on it, when it has affected you and changed you. So Jesus is really saying, "He who acts on truth will be given more; but he who has it and doesn't act on it will lose it. And what is more, he will lose the very capacity to receive truth." This is his warning. And he said to the disciples, "To you it has been given to know," because they were the kind of people who acted on truth. So he starts to explain this parable to them:

> "Hear then the parable of the sower. When any one hears the word of the kingdom and does not understand it, the evil one comes and snatches away what is sown in his heart; this is what was sown along the path" (Matt. 13:18–19).

Each of the elements of the story has an explanation, a corresponding truth connected with it. Our Lord begins to explain it section by section—the way he wants us to study all these parables. He begins with the seed. You notice that he does not say anything specific about who the sower is, although in the next parable he does. The important thing to notice here is what the seed is. Jesus says it is "the word of the kingdom," that is, the word about the existence of an invisible spiritual kingdom all around us which is very essential to us and from which all our lives are governed and to which they all must relate.

That is the great truth which God wants us to know —that all of life is not contained in what you can see and touch and taste and hear and smell. Those senses open up a certain range of experience to you, but there is more to life than that. There is an invisible kingdom beyond what you can apprehend with your five senses. It is very real—as real as anything you can see or touch. And in that kingdom are hidden all the answers to the problems with which we wrestle. It is essential, therefore, that we understand this kingdom exists. But more than that, the word of the kingdom is that from this source, invisible and unseen, comes all which man desperately needs and is searching for in life. That is the good news of the gospel. The word of the kingdom, then, is the gospel.

MIGHTIER THAN ROME

When the Apostle Paul wrote to the Romans, he told them how eager he was to come to their city. He hungered to come and declare the gospel to them. Despite the might, power, and influence centered in Rome at that time, Paul said, "I am not ashamed of the gospel." And well he might not have been ashamed, for in it, as he says, are the two things men need most desperately: the power of God, and the righteousness of God (Rom. 1:16–17).

Power is the *ability* to do, to accomplish. Every person in the world today is seeking that kind of power— the secret of adequacy, the ability to be and do what you would like to be and do, the ability to cope with life, to handle whatever life throws at you. The most fundamental, urgent cry of any human heart, anywhere, is somehow to find the secret of this power.

Righteousness is the *freedom* to do. It means that the individual has all his internal problems solved. He is released, no longer hung up with problems and inhibitions, limitations and barriers within. These are solved and removed. He is no longer under the burden of guilt nor defeated by self-loathing. He is free to be and to accomplish what God wants. So, both the ability and the freedom to accomplish God's will in our lives are available in the gospel.

That is the seed being sown during the whole course

of this age. This is the age of sowing the seed of the word of promise of the power and the righteousness of God. That wonderful, attractive, powerful seed is being dropped into human hearts everywhere, and the sowing started with Jesus. He was the first great Sower who went out with this word, but millions have followed him since, sowing this seed wherever they go. It may be in the form of a simple Christian testimony. It may be in an elaborate sermon or in a book that someone reads. It may be just a word, a single phrase dropped into a conversation, which takes root and changes that whole life. Perhaps you are one of many who can testify that the thing which arrested you and turned you around and changed you was just a phrase which somebody uttered. This seed is powerful.

The crux of the parable concerns the condition of the soils into which this seed is dropped. This is what our Lord wants us to comprehend. There are various kinds of soils, he says, upon which the Word can fall. The soil, of course, is the human heart. Wherever the Word is sown four kinds of soil are usually present, four conditions of the human heart to which this Word speaks. Our Lord wants us to see what they are.

JUST A PASSING THOUGHT

What is the trouble with this first heart? Jesus says, "When any one hears the word of the kingdom and does not understand it, the evil one comes [the birds are a symbol of the evil one] and snatches away what is sown in his heart; this is what was sown along the path" (Matt. 13:19). This first kind of individual has a heart which is hard and narrow like a path trodden down by the traffic of human feet crossing a field. In his explanation, Jesus focuses upon what causes this condition. The word comes, he says, but they do not understand it. The idea is not that they could not understand, but that they do not try. They don't take the time to understand. Now, what kind of a heart is this? You can see that this is what we might call the materialistic heart, the kind of person who does not want to be bothered with thinking about anything beyond what he can see and hear and smell and touch and taste. This is the humanistic heart, the liberal heart, or even the atheistic heart.

Here is a man who has been rendered momentarily thoughtful by the word of the kingdom. Something has challenged him for the moment to think about God and about life. And for a moment he wonders, "Maybe there is something to this." He has received a passing impression, but it requires more thought, more self-evaluation—and he does not want to be bothered. So he shrugs it off. And immediately our Lord says, the enemy comes—Satan, the evil one—and snatches away the thought from his heart, and it never comes back again. So he goes on untroubled, thinking that the world remains the way he has conceived it to be.

There are many people like this who live on these terms. C. S. Lewis, in his book *The Screwtape Letters,* describes a man who goes into the British Museum and sits down to read certain books that are there. Something he reads suggests to him a thought about

God, and he is inspired to think of him. For a moment it looks as though he is really going to think this idea through. But then Screwtape manages to divert him with the thought that it is time for lunch and that he would be in much better shape to tackle this important subject after he has eaten. Screwtape goes on to say,

> Once he was in the street the battle was won. I showed him a newsboy shouting the midday paper, and a No. 73 bus going past, and before he reached the bottom of the steps I had got into him an unalterable conviction that, whatever odd ideas might come into a man's head when he was shut up alone with his books, a healthy dose of 'real life' (by which he meant the bus and the newsboy) was enough to show him that all 'that sort of thing' just couldn't be true.

That is the kind of soil Jesus is talking about. The devil takes care of him, brainwashes him. The thought is snatched away if it is not dealt with then—and it never returns again. There are many like that. They have settled for a world bounded on the north by their work, on the south by their family, on the east by taxes, and on the west by death. That is the whole of life to them. They have been described in the little jingle that goes,

> Into this world to eat and to sleep,
> And to know no reason why he was born
> Save to consume the corn,
> Devour the cattle, flock, and fish,
> And leave behind an empty dish.

And that's it. That's all. That's life. When the word of the kingdom falls upon that kind of heart, it causes a momentary impression. But it is immediately shrugged off because it is different, it is challenging, it awakens the possibility of an entire world he has never thought of. But he is comfortable where he is, so he divests himself of it and the enemy comes and takes it away and it is gone.

And yet, remarkably enough, it was this very verse that reached John Bunyan and led him to Christ. That blasphemous tinker of Bedford was known as the most godless man in his village. He was regarded as so hardhearted and committed to godlessness that no Christian had any hope for him at all. But he heard this story of the sower, and these very words seized upon his heart. And he said to himself, "Even the devil knows that if a man believes the Word he'll be saved!" So he believed it and he *was* saved. He became the author of *Pilgrim's Progress* and a tremendous testimony for God in his age.

SEASONAL PEOPLE

Let's look now at the second heart condition our Lord describes:

> As for what was sown on rocky ground, this is he who hears the word and immediately receives it with joy; yet he has no root in himself, but endures for a while, and when tribulation or persecution arises on account of the word, immediately he falls away (Matt. 13:20–21).

What is the matter with this heart? The ground is described as rocky, but that doesn't mean soil containing a lot of rocks. The idea here is that there are a few inches of earth on top of a broad shelf of bedrock. In other words this is shallow soil, thinly spread over a ledge of bedrock. The key our Lord gives us here is that "he has no root in himself." This is what we would call a shallow life, one that flits from one experience to another, never content with anything for very long. This heart is always on the prowl, restless, searching, groping. You have met people like that—faddists, enthusiasts for the gospel this week ("Oh, what a wonderful thing this is!") and next week it is Geritol, or vitamin Z that has taken their fancy. The word our Lord uses to describe this kind of person is, literally, "seasonal"; they believe the gospel when it's in season.

Many people like that are being reached right now. For example, among the tens of thousands of young people who are turning to Christ in our day there are a lot who will drop out when the season changes. They will not continue because they live on the surface; there is no depth in their life, nothing goes deep into their heart. When the gospel reaches people like this, they receive it with joy. As long as it is a warm, glorious day for the word, they are enthusiastic. But when the season turns cold and stormy, and tribulation and persecution come, immediately they are gone. They wither and die.

Thus our Lord illustrates the terrible danger of a shallow heart. The devil took care of the first kind of man, but the flesh takes care of this one. Because he never allows the word to take root, never learns to depend on the power of Christ in him, the emotional trials and seasons of testing will easily uproot him.

NOT ENOUGH ROOM

Now here is the third type of heart:

> As for what was sown among thorns, this is he who hears the word, but the cares of the world and the delight in riches choke the word, and it proves unfruitful (Matt. 13:22).

Here is the typical American businessman and his wife. What is the trouble? Busyness, that's all. It is not that he is uninterested; on the contrary, he *is* interested in the gospel. It is not that he is shallow; he isn't. He is very capable of thinking in depth and analyzing issues. He does it in business; she does it in her social life. The trouble is that he wants it all. He wants the fruitfulness of life that comes from the gospel, but with it he also wants everything else. He wants the so-called "finer things" of life. We describe him as trying to keep up with the Joneses. (That means buying things you don't need with money you don't have to impress people you don't even like.) He wants a color TV set and a swimming pool and a fine home and two beautiful cars and a full social life. The result is that he has no time to think about the Word, no time to receive it and meditate. He is too wrapped up with the cares of this world and the pursuit of things.

When my daughters were younger, one of them used to like to go riding with me in the car, but she always wanted to take all her "friends." I don't mean the neighborhood children. Her friends were her teddy bear and her stuffed rabbit and her dolls and some other toys. When I'd ask her to go, she would run and grab the bear and the rabbit and three dolls and several other kinds of toys, and with her arms filled, she would try to get into the car. But there wasn't room for them all, and so she had to choose between me and her friends. I guess I won most of the time, but she was too intent upon taking everything with her.

That is what is happening with people today. They want it all. They want everything that the world can offer and everything God can offer. But the remarkable thing about the Word is that God will never settle on those terms. He is always saying, ". . . seek first his kingdom and his righteousness, and all these things shall be yours as well" (Matt. 6:33); and ". . . what will it profit a man, if he gains the whole world and forfeits his life?" (Matt. 16:26).

THE FRUITFUL LIFE

At last we come to the fourth soil, which is the good soil:

> As for what was sown on good soil, this is he who hears the word and understands it; he indeed bears fruit, and yields, in one case a hundredfold, in another sixty, and in another thirty (Matt. 13:23).

Notice the qualities of this type of person. Here is a heart that is neither hard and narrow nor flippant. He understands the Word; he thinks about it, ponders over it. He receives it gladly, but his life is not shallow. He bears fruit. The seed remains long enough to sprout and grow and to come to fruition. Finally, his fruit is not lost in a jumble of things, the thorns and thistles of life, but he brings forth varying amounts

The seed comes to fruition with varying degrees of harvest, depending on differing circumstances, times, and seasons. However, in any case the fruit is there.

SOWING IS NOT SALVATION

The key point of this whole parable is that the only one of these four hearts which is genuinely Christian is the fourth one. The sowing is not salvation. Nor is the hearing of the Word. Many hear, but they are not Christians. Even the sprouting of the seed is not salvation—that is important to note. The enthusiasm, the joy with which it is received, the immediate results in the life, are not yet salvation. Isn't that startling? There are many who profess in this way, Jesus said, but they are not Christians. Salvation is seen when the fruit appears. This happens when the will is genuinely yielded to the lordship of Christ, when the Word is welcomed and nourished and acted on and allowed to grow to fruition.

But we need to note here that our Lord is describing hearts, not lives. He is not saying that once a man is like a certain kind of soil he is unchangeable, that his *life* is forever like this. His *heart* may be like this, but hearts change. Hearts are altered by the circumstances of our life. And it is quite possible that a single individual can pass through all four of these conditions. Probably all of us do. What Jesus is asking us is, "What is your heart like when it hears the Word? What are you like when the Word of the kingdom, with its promise of power and of righteousness, falls on your heart? What is your heart like then?"

If your heart is in any of these unsatisfactory conditions—hard or shallow or distracted or resistant in any way—it is possible for your heart to be brought to God because God is able to change it, whatever its condition. He is the Creator. He is able to break up the hard heart, just as he did with John Bunyan. He is able to deepen the shallow life. He is able to slow up the over-busy life so that the wonderful, living, life-producing Word may take root in your heart and change you and introduce you to the power and the righteousness of God.

What a picture this is of our age! The sowing has been going on constantly throughout the age, but the enemies of the gospel—the world, the flesh, and the devil—have been at work as well, as this parable illustrates. The devil is the one who lies to us, who tells us that life consists only of what we can detect with our senses and that nothing lies beyond that. That is the devil at work to deceive and destroy us. The flesh is that tendency in us to relate only to the passing moment, to the changing scene, to the surface of life, involving our emotions in such a way that all we are concerned about is how we are feeling at the moment. Our mood forms the basis for our decisions. That is the destructive principle of the flesh at work. The world is that which engages us in busyness, in trying to amass riches, involving us with the cares of this life, with the preservation of possessions. Our attention becomes centered upon things instead of people, upon material wealth instead of personal fellowship and spiritual relationship. This is the world at work to destroy us.

But as the Word of God falls upon us, the question each of us must ask is, "What is my heart like now?" And with that our Lord leaves this parable with us, for us to answer that question in the depths of our own hearts.

Heavenly Father, we ask that you will take our hearts, whatever they are like right at this moment, and make them good soil, responsive, ready to listen, ready to think, ready to pay attention. Let your word remain in our hearts. Let us ponder what we have heard, think more deeply than we ever have before, and ask ourselves, "What does this Word mean? How does it affect me?" The Word must be constantly received. It continually drops upon us, continually seeks to bear fruit. Lord, take our hearts and make them into good soil for the Word. We ask it in Jesus' name, Amen.

3

The Case of the
Mysterious Harvest

One of the issues which has been debated for centuries concerning our world and the course of this age
is the question: Is the world getting better or is it getting worse? And, depending on when you asked that
question, you would find a majority of voices raised
on one side or the other. At the beginning of this century you would have been laughed almost to scorn if
you had suggested that the world is getting worse instead of better. Today it is the other way around. Now
it is almost ridiculous to suggest that the world is getting better, although there are some who still hold this
view. The other day I ran across a rather humorous
statement of it:

> Now granddad, viewing earth's worn cogs,
> Said, "Things were going to the dogs."

45

> His granddad, in his house of logs,
> Said, "Things were going to the dogs."
> And his granddad, in the Flemish bogs,
> Said, "Things were going to the dogs."
> And his granddad, in his old skin togs,
> Said, "Things were going to the dogs."
> There's one thing I have to state:
> The dogs have had a good long wait.

That is the philosophy which suggests that the world, if not improving, is at least not getting any worse. But our Lord has given us a key to the understanding of that great question in this parable of the wheat and the weeds; it is one of the secrets of the kingdom of heaven. The parable begins:

Another parable he put before them, saying, "The kingdom of heaven may be compared to a man who sowed good seed in his field; but while men were sleeping, his enemy came and sowed weeds among the wheat, and went away. So when the plants came up and bore grain, then the weeds appeared also. And the servants of the householder came and said to him, 'Sir, did you not sow good seed in your field? How then has it weeds?' He said to them, 'An enemy has done this.' The servants said to him, 'Then do you want us to go and gather them?' But he said, 'No; lest in gathering the weeds you root up the wheat along with them. Let both grow together until the harvest; and at harvest time I will tell the reapers, Gather the weeds first and bind them in bundles to be burned, but gather the wheat into my barn'" (Matt. 13:24–30).

In this story are hidden some wonderfully helpful clues to the understanding of the age in which we live. As Matthew goes on to tell us, Jesus spoke two more parables and then there came a break (probably a coffee break). He left the crowds and went into the house, and there his disciples came and asked him about the meaning of the parable. Beginning with verse 36 we have our Lord's explanation. So let's go back over the parable section by section and examine it in the light of the explanation.

ANOTHER KIND OF SEED

You notice that this too is a parable of sowing. But the sowing is quite different from that in the first parable. There, you remember, the seed was the Word of God, and the sowing was to go on throughout the entire age. Wherever the Word of God was to be sown it would fall on four different kinds of soils, four kinds of hearts, and in one it would take root and grow up. That has been happening now for twenty centuries. But in this parable the seed is not the Word of God. It is what Jesus in his explanation calls "the sons of the kingdom":

> Then he left the crowds and went into the house. And his disciples came to him, saying, "Explain to us the parable of the weeds of the field." He answered, "He who sows the good seed is the Son of man [Jesus himself]; the field is the world, and the good seed means the sons of the kingdom; the weeds are the sons of the evil one, and the enemy who sowed them is the devil . . ." (Matt. 13:36–39).

So the seed sown here is not ideas, not the Word of Scripture, not the word of the gospel, but people. However, this does link up with the first parable. The ones which were produced by the good seed of the

Word in the first parable are now in turn taken by the Lord and scattered throughout the world. That is the picture we have here. But this is a quite different sowing. The first one goes on continuously; this one only once, at the beginning of the age. Yet it reproduces itself all through this age. In the first parable we were looking at the soils; here we are looking at the whole field which Jesus says is the world.

It is important to notice how the Lord begins this parable. Do not, as many do in reading this series of parables, make the mistake of taking the very first thing he relates to the kingdom as being the entire comparison. No, it is the whole picture that he has in view. The kingdom of heaven is *not* like a man who sowed good seed in his field. Rather, the whole story must be included to be a picture of the kingdom of heaven. God's work and God's operations in the world of our day is the kingdom of heaven. The Greek text here literally means the kingdom of heaven "has become like" this. The Word had already been sown in the hearts of individuals, as Jesus described in the first parable. Some of the seed fell on good ground and brought forth fruit and transformed those individuals so that they became sons of the kingdom. Then, in this parable, Jesus says he now takes these sons of the kingdom and scatters them throughout the world. He is predicting what will happen in the course of history as God is at work in human events.

We find the historical fulfillment of this in the Book of Acts. This is how he began this age. You remember that at the close of the Gospels Jesus gathered with his disciples and said to them, "Go therefore and make disciples of all nations, baptizing them in the name of the Father and of the Son and of the Holy Spirit, teaching them to observe all that I have commanded you; and lo, I am with you always, to the close of the age" (Matt. 28:19–20). That "great commission" was the beginning of the scattering of these sons of the kingdom throughout the world. As you read on in the Book of Acts, on the day of Pentecost the Holy Spirit came and empowered the waiting disciples, filling them with himself. Then, a little later on, persecution arose and the disciples were scattered everywhere, preaching the Word. That is the sowing our Lord is talking about here; he scattered them throughout the world. And Paul, in his letter to the Colossians, recognizes this. In the first chapter he says,

> Of this you have heard before in the word of the truth, the gospel which has come to you, as indeed in the whole world it is bearing fruit and growing . . . (Col. 1:5–6)

THE FIELD IS THE WORLD

In this parable, it is essential to notice that the field represents not the church, but the world. These sons of the kingdom are put where God wants them—in the world. Wherever you are, as a child of God, as a son of the kingdom by faith in Jesus Christ, you have been put there by the Lord Jesus. It is so important to understand that he has sown you and put you where you are. The church is to gather together for worship, for instruction, and for mutual fellowship, but then it is to go out. There is a kind of a rhythm of life within the church—it comes together, then goes out again, scattered out into the world. And wherever you are out there is where the word of witness is given, where the truth of the Word is promulgated. That is what the Lord has in mind here. The field, therefore, is the world, the human race, society, as we normally term it. In that world of humanity the Lord Jesus has scattered his own.

Now into that same field, Jesus says, there came an enemy. He came right at the beginning of this age, and he came while men were sleeping, unaware of what was happening. Out of sheer malice and hatred he sowed a crop of his own which the Revised Standard Version calls "weeds." Literally, it is the plant which today is called "darnel," a poisonous weed which looks very much like wheat. In fact, when it first begins to grow even an expert cannot distinguish it from wheat. But as it grows, it begins to change. And, finally, when it comes to harvest, even a child can tell that it is not wheat. The Jews called it "degenerate wheat" or, literally, "bastard wheat," because it appears to be wheat but it is not. That is the figure that our Lord employs. These are also persons that are sown. They are what Jesus calls "the sons of the evil one." They, too, have been scattered throughout the human race by the enemy—and especially *among the wheat.* We will see more about that in a moment.

TEACHERS OF EVIL

I know that there is a sense in which the whole world, as the Scriptures tell us, is under the control of satanic philosophy and thought. Jesus referred to the devil as the ruler of this world because he governs the thinking of people. But in the light of this parable I think it is wrong to think of everybody in the world—men, women, and children alike—as "sons of the evil one." Jesus never called anybody a son of the devil except the Pharisees who were teachers of evil in the name of righteousness. He used the term to refer to someone who pretended to be religiously correct but was actually disseminating error.

It is true that we are all members of a fallen race. We are all born into this world tainted with Adam's sin so that we all tend toward evil naturally. No one has to teach you how to lie. Did you ever go to school to learn that? Do you have a diploma to show that you have successfully accomplished training in how to be selfish? No, you learn all this naturally. You never have to be trained in how to be dishonest, how to cheat, how to be a hypocrite. We are all natural hypocrites, and experts at it, because we are members of a fallen race. But babies could hardly be called "sons of the evil one" in the sense our Lord intends here.

I remember that Dr. H. A. Ironside once described a rather stern and austere pastor who went to see a woman. She was showing him her baby, holding the infant up so he could see how beautiful it was. This pastor drew a long face and said to her, "Madam, what a pity that this little one should be a child of the devil!" Well, that is hardly the way to make a hit with the mother—nor is it theologically correct. It is true that the child is in a world dominated by satanic thought and that as he grows, he will probably become more and more possessed with wrong ideas and concepts. Because he may be totally unaware they are wrong he may gradually become committed to these evil principles, but it is only at that point that he might be called a "son of the evil one." But what Jesus evidently has in mind here are the teachers of evil under the guise of religion.

Let's pull this first part of the parable together now: Jesus thinks of the whole human race as a field, bleak and lifeless. At the beginning he scattered in it men committed to him, men and women in whom the truth of the Word had taken root and had come alive. He thrust them out into the field, scattering them here and there in order that they might reproduce themselves and yield men committed to him. Then Satan came and did the same thing, deliberately scattering certain evil teachers who appear to be religious and righteous. Jesus began by scattering men committed to the word of truth in order to produce more like himself. Satan began by scattering men committed to the lie in order to produce more like himself. And so both grow together now until the harvest. See how they grow; Jesus said,

> So when the plants came up and bore grain, then the weeds appeared also. And the servants of the householder came and said to him, 'Sir, did you not sow good seed in your field? How then has it weeds?' He said to them, 'An enemy has done this' (Matt. 13:26–28).

He implies here that those who are his servants will become troubled by the sight of these weeds in the field because they will be growing among the wheat. It is important that you see that. Our Lord said that these weeds would be sown not just in the world in general but among the wheat, that is, in the church, and that they would grow up within the church. So the wheat are true believers, and the weeds are those who appear to be true believers but who are actually false. The two are so intermingled that at first you can't tell them apart—until the fruit begins to appear. Remember when the Apostle Paul was speaking to the elders of the church at Ephesus, he told them,

> I know that after my departure fierce wolves will come in among you, not sparing the flock; and from among *your own selves* will arise men speaking perverse things, to draw away the disciples after them (Acts 20:29–30, emphasis mine).

That is the sowing our Lord is talking about here, and Paul's words fit the historical picture exactly. In the early centuries of this age it was very difficult to tell true Christians from false. If you read the writings of the early church fathers from the first two or three centuries, you find them hard to classify. Many of them were obviously godly, genuinely, born-again, and regenerate men who loved God. And yet they sometimes taught errors and heresies right along with the truth, and they were just as strong for the error as they were for the truth. It is rather disconcerting to read these men. You would think we might find a pure fountain of truth in the early centuries, but we do not.

Gradually the great central truths of the faith began to be debated and there was a great deal of doctrinal controversy. But as the truth grew, it gradually became apparent that the heresies were leading men astray while the truth was establishing them. Gradually the weeds began to emerge in their true form, becoming recognizable as weeds—teachers of error. It was then that the truths of the church were crystallized into the creeds that are familiar to many today—the Nicean Creed, the Apostles' Creed—these are statements of the truth devised in order to counteract the heresy that was rampant within the church.

LEAVE THE WEEDS ALONE

Then during the so-called Dark Ages you find the next step described by our Lord:

> The servants said to him, "Then do you want us to go and gather them?" But he said, "No; lest in gathering the weeds you root up the wheat along with them. Let both grow together until the harvest . . ." (Matt. 13:28–29).

"Let both grow together until the harvest." That is our Lord's word. It is amazing how many Christians ignore these words of Jesus and are constantly trying to purify the church in ways unwarranted by the Scriptures. In the great awakening we are seeing today many young people are making this mistake again. They say they are going to go off and start their own church, and it is going to be a true church, a pure church. There will be no heresy in it. And so you find splinter groups calling themselves the "True Church," the "One Way," the "Only Way," and so forth. They say they have the truth and no one else does. But that is impossible. Jesus said that you cannot do it that way. You cannot separate evil from the church. You cannot even *drive* it out. It is going to be there in some form. This doesn't mean that we are not to expose it and meet it positively with the teaching of the truth. We are. Nor are we to allow those who exhibit clear forms of error to take leadership within the church. Other Scripture helps us here. But what our Lord wants us to understand is that no human effort is going to eliminate error from the church. "Let them both grow together," he said.

In order to realize how completely intermingled error is with truth, just look into your own heart. No one person is completely true and pure and perfect. I even have a little error in myself. I don't see it . . . but my wife does, and it breaks in upon my own astonished gaze from time to time. It is there, so how are you going to get rid of it in the church? That's just it; Jesus says you cannot get rid of it. You will find that it is *there,* and it is going to stay *there,* and no human effort will be able to eliminate it. Therefore, all the efforts to try to form a pure church, or a pure council of churches, are doomed to failure before they begin, as Jesus has pointed out.

Many such attempts to purify the church have happened in history. In the fourth and fifth century there were godly men who honestly advocated the overthrow of heretics with the sword and with fire. And yet notice in the parable how our Lord restrains his true servants. He told them not to do anything like this. But throughout the Middle Ages, when both truth and error in this form were growing together,

evil in the name of religion became more and more
apparent. Finally, its true nature began to be very
evident to people when thousands were perishing at
the hands of evil in the name of religion. That is what
finally caused the Protestant Reformation.

But even honest servants of God at that time won-
dered if perhaps they should in turn kill those who had
persecuted Christians in the name of religion. Luther
once said to one of the Catholic emissaries, Emser,
"If heretics have deserved the stake, then you and the
Pope should be killed a thousand times. Nevertheless,
I do not want it to be done." You can see how the
Spirit of Christ within him restrained him from going
over into this error. Unfortunately, such was not
always the case. John Calvin ultimately consented to
the burning of a heretic named Servetus, and Protestants in general have dealt wrongly with heretics from
time to time.

What is the Lord's plan for handling this problem?
He says, "Let them both grow together until the harvest." That is, "Don't worry about it, I'll take care of
it. I've got my own plan for handling this and nothing
you can do will eliminate the problem (as has proven
true in history). But don't worry about it. Keep your
message positive, preach the Word, teach the truth,
deal with it in your own hearts, exclude it from leadership, but don't try to eliminate error. Don't launch a
crusade that exists only for the purpose of trying to
wipe out evil or error, particularly religious error, because you won't succeed."

This is the mistake made by many of the separatist

movements of our day. Billy Graham is often under attack from them because he recognizes that there *is* error in the churches and he does not have the ability to distinguish whether a man is genuinely a Christian or not. So until he can see this clearly by his fruit, he accepts him at face value. There are some who attack him viciously because of this, pretending that they have the ability to make this distinction, while the Lord said that no one could.

COUNTERFEIT APOSTLES

There are sons of the evil one in every church. There are some who claim to be Christian, who talk like Christians, who act like Christians outwardly, but who have never yielded their lives to the Lord Jesus Christ. They are representatives of the doctrines of demons, seducing spirits, as the Apostle Paul calls them, teaching wrong ideas that have infiltrated society. A major point of this parable is to give us a clue to the way the enemy works most successfully. It is by imitation, by counterfeit. How simple it would be if evil people would only *look* evil. Wouldn't that help a lot? If hypocrites would only snarl and growl a little, it would help so much. But they always look so pleasant and talk so sweetly. They are such nice people that we easily go along with their ideas. We cannot believe that such nice people could be so far wrong. And unless we use the Word of God to evaluate their teachings we can be deceived by the niceness of people who are imitation, counterfeit apostles, as the Word of God calls them.

Now look at the way the Lord plans to deal with them: " '. . . at harvest time I will tell the reapers, Gather the weeds first and bind them in bundles to be burned, but gather the wheat into my barn' " (Matt. 13:30). He explains that, beginning in verse 39:

> . . . the harvest is the close of the age, and the reapers are angels. Just as the weeds are gathered and burned with fire, so will it be at the close of the age. The Son of man will send his angels, and they will gather out of his kingdom all causes of sin and all evildoers, and throw them into the furnace of fire; there men will weep and gnash their teeth. Then the righteous will shine like the sun in the kingdom of their Father. He who has ears, let him hear (Matt. 13:39–43).

Our Lord here is looking ahead to his return in power and glory at the close of this age. In Matthew 24 and 25 you have the great message our Lord gave about what it will be like at the end of the age. It is a time of great tribulation, of terrible judgment on the earth. Many Bible scholars deduce from the Book of Daniel that it probably will be about seven years in length. It is the time covered by the greater part of the Book of Revelation. Each visitation of judgment in Revelation is like a swing of an angel's scythe as he goes through the harvest field, reaping the harvest of earth. In fact, the Book of Revelation employs that very imagery, saying, "The hour to reap has come, for the harvest of the earth is fully ripe" (Rev. 14:15).

When Jesus sends forth his angels it will not be something visible. Angelic activity goes on behind the scenes, so there will not be a sudden appearance of angels in the presence of men. He is describing here the activities that will take place in human affairs for which men will not be able to account, for which they will not have any explanation.

The Lord said that the reapers would go forth and bind the weeds into bundles, literally, "with a view toward burning." That is, the burning is not to take place immediately when the binding does. It is to come at the end, at the close of the age. What our Lord is saying will happen is that as we near the close of the age, we will see men of evil gathering themselves together into great associations of evil. That is the work of angels. They are binding the weeds together into bundles for the time of burning, the time of judgment that is to follow. And there are many, looking at our age, who say that this is where we are today, that we are seeing a great clumping together of those of like mind who hold to evil principles and tendencies (especially those who do so in the name of religion), and that as we near the time of the end of the age, there seems to be a growing tendency toward the association of evil persons who will ultimately be swept away in judgment.

THE FATHER'S BARN

But the wheat is to be gathered into the Father's barn. Now, there is no time schedule in this parable. You cannot tell when this is to happen in relation to other events. It is simply mentioned and left there. But that is the destiny of the wheat. And Jesus says, "Then the righteous will shine like the sun in the kingdom of their Father" (Matt. 13:43). In the Book of Revelation John sees a great multitude from every tribe and nation standing before God and appearing to shine as the sun in the kingdom of the Father. They have come out of the great tribulation, the harvest of the earth— men and women who had laid down their lives during that time. And all through this age this is what has been happening. Men and women have been laying down their lives in death—but not necessarily violent death. Jesus' word to all Christians is "Be faithful unto death." That simply means you are to remain true to him until you die. This is the sign that you really belong to him.

Then at last, as John goes on to say, the kingdom of the world will become the kingdom of our Lord and of his Christ. Then will come the time to which all the prophets have looked forward, when the earth will blossom like the rose and men will beat their swords into plowshares and their spears into pruning hooks, and there will be no more war across the face of the earth. But that kind of peace cannot be worked out by men; it awaits the solution of God.

BETTER AND WORSE

Now let's return to answer the question with which we began. Is the world getting better or is it getting worse? The answer our Lord gives is clearly, "Both!" Good men are getting better, more powerful, more constructive, and evil men are getting worse, more powerful, more destructive. The two sowings are growing up to a harvest side by side. If evil is getting worse, God is matching it with a demonstration of his power and with the increase of good. That is why I think it is logical to expect that as we near the end of the age, and increasingly see evil amassing itself and breaking out in tremendous authority and power, we will also see the Spirit of God breaking out in authority and power among groups of people. An awakening will occur right along with the deepening decline into darkness and evil. That is what is happening in our own day, and Jesus says it will go on until the harvest. And when the harvest of earth comes at the end of the age God will begin to reap—the good to be his, the evil to be destroyed.

Now, where do you stand? Is the seed of the Word of God growing in your heart? Are you a son of the kingdom, and, therefore, an influence for good throughout the earth? Or are you a son of the evil one, beginning to spread lies, deceptive concepts, and to spread abroad the destructive philosophies that are so widespread in the world today. It is a lie of Satan that man can live by himself, that he is self-sufficient, that he is able to carry on his own affairs, that he can run his own life and, therefore, does not need God. That is the great lie which always marks the philosophy of the devil. Or are you one of the sons of the kingdom whom God is using in this day to bring this great harvest to fruition and produce that which will glorify and delight his heart throughout all time?

Our heavenly Father, we thank you for your truth. How it searches us out! How it sets our age into perspective and makes us see life as it really is. Teach us, Lord, to value the truth as it is in

Jesus, the truth revealed to us by that One who
loved us enough to give himself for us. We can
trust the One who died for our sakes and who
lives to live within us. We thank you for that.
We pray that we may be sons of the kingdom
today, teachers of truth, openers of eyes, helping
men out of their darkness. For the glory of the
gospel is that even those who are becoming sons
of the evil one can be changed into sons of the
kingdom. And you have come to make this
dividing mark in history. Help us, Lord, to see
ourselves as we are in relation to it. In Jesus'
name, Amen.

4

The Case

of the Ambitious Seed

Now we come to the third of the remarkable parables which our Lord called the secrets, the mysteries, of the kingdom of heaven. In this third parable we have another story of a sowing and of its results in human history:

> Another parable he put before them, saying, "The kingdom of heaven is like a grain of mustard seed which a man took and sowed in his field; it is the smallest of all seeds, but when it has grown it is the greatest of shrubs and becomes a tree, so that the birds of the air come and make nests in its branches" (Matt. 13:31–32).

I want to stress again that these seven parables are all part of one message. Our Lord interpreted the first two for us as a guide to our own interpretation of the rest. He gave us a start, and he expects us to continue in the same direction. It is clear from the first two that every element in the story has significance. Each is symbolic of some factor or movement in history. As he unfolded the meanings to us, we saw what the seed meant, what the sowing was, what the soils were, what the wheat and weeds stood for, and who the reapers were. All of these became clear as he interpreted them. This is the first parable of the series which does not have an interpretation from our Lord's lips. So he expects us, obviously, to go on applying the same principles he gave in the first two, and to understand the others from the symbols he employed there as well as from other symbols in Scripture.

CONSISTENT SYMBOLS

One of the basic laws in reading the Bible is that Scripture never uses a symbol in two conflicting ways; they are used consistently throughout. This is very important for you to know. Learn how Scripture uses a symbol and then employs it the same way wherever it appears. Then you will come out with a clear understanding of what the Scripture is teaching. We must do that here. Men have wasted their lives trying to accomplish what they call "bringing in the kingdom" by a false interpretation of this very parable and of the one that follows it, the parable of the leaven. They have misjudged the whole movement of history because by a mistaken use of the symbols they have misunderstood what our Lord is saying. So it is important that we view each parable here in its context and allow the Lord's interpretation to guide us.

In this parable you will notice that five symbols are used. There is the sower again, the field in which he sowed, and the seed that is sown, which in this case is mustard seed. There is the tree which grows from it and the birds that make their nests in its branches. As with the other parables, Jesus intends that we understand what these symbols mean in terms of what has been happening in the world since that day. So we will look at it with that in mind.

It is easy to interpret the first two symbols. The sower obviously is our Lord himself. In each of these parables he has been sowing, and in the second parable he told us, "The sower is the son of man." He sowed in the field, that is, he planted the seed in the world; the field is the world, society, the whole of mankind.

This is the third sowing which occurs in these parables, and in each one a different seed is sown. The use of these various seeds is our Lord's way of indicating various aspects of the great message which he turned loose in the world. He sowed a fantastic, revolutionary, radical, word in human society. In one case it is like wheat which, if received in good soil, will grow up to a true harvest. In another case it is actually people, "the sons of the kingdom." It is an incarnation, the Word become flesh, and these people are placed here and there throughout the world wherever the Lord wants them. But in this case the Word is like a mustard seed.

THE QUALITIES OF MUSTARD

Why mustard seed? Our Lord employed a symbol here which he expected these people to understand. Mustard is a peculiar kind of seed. It has an unusual quality, and this is what our Lord wanted them to catch. What do you think was the first thing these disciples thought of when they heard this symbol employed? Very likely, they thought of mustard in the same way we do. Mustard has the quality of pungency; it is biting, irritating, and disturbing.

When I was a boy growing up in Montana, we lived in a little town forty-two miles from the nearest doctor. We didn't have any electricity or plumbing, but we were quite happy without all the modern conveniences. However, when we got sick, we couldn't call for a doctor. There wasn't even a drugstore in town. We had to rely upon what we called "home remedies." If you got a cough or pneumonia or chest congestion, there was a standard remedy to apply. We used what we called a "mustard plaster," which is a gooey mixture of mustard and water smeared on a cloth and placed right on the chest. After it has been there about five minutes, you can feel it begin to burn, and you start itching and squirming. The contest is to see which will wear out first, the mustard plaster or you. You are supposed to hold it on until your skin turns as red as a berry. I don't think it ever cured anything, but it made you forget what was wrong.

That quality of mustard has been well known from the very earliest times. It was known to be an irritant, something fiery and biting, stirring up the blood. When Darius, the king of the Persians, invaded Europe with a great army, he was met by Alexander the Great. Darius sent Alexander a bag of sesame seed as a kind of taunt, indicating by the number of these small seeds the vast multitude of soldiers he had at his command. When Alexander received it, he sent back by the same messenger a bag of mustard seed by way of saying, "You may be many, but we're tough and biting and pungent. We can handle you." And they did. That is the character of mustard and these people knew that. So our Lord is using a very apt symbol by which he indicates that the message of the kingdom of God is intended to be arousing, irritating, and disturbing among men. Turn it loose and it will get a whole community excited, stirred up, either negatively or positively, as we see it working so beautifully today.

In a nearby city there is a church which I have been watching with great interest. For all its history, some seventy years or more, this church had been liberally oriented. It had never taught the Bible, never believed in the supernatural. Its members had never understood the great gospel message. They had been concerned with social problems and moral standards and that sort of thing, but had never known anything of the power of God. But a year or so ago, through an unusual chain of circumstances, the pastor became a real Christian and he started preaching the gospel. It is most interesting to watch what is happening in the congregation. He is making a lot of people uncomfortable. They are beginning to squirm and itch—you can see the mustard working on them. Others are being healed and rejoicing in it. The pastor is doing a very gracious, loving job of proclaiming this great message, but its quality is obvious—it is pungent and biting and burning.

A PROVERB OF SMALLNESS

Our Lord calls particular attention to another property of mustard. It is, he says, the smallest of all seeds. If you have seen a mustard seed you know that although it is small, it is obviously not the smallest of all seeds. There are seeds smaller than mustard seeds, and these were present even in Palestine in our Lord's day. Many have been disturbed by this, wondering how our Lord could understand so little about agriculture. But here, if we put ourselves back into those times, we learn that there was a common proverb which used the mustard seed as a symbol of smallness or insignificance. "Small as a mustard seed," they would say. We do the same today. We say something is "as small as a flea." Certainly there are smaller things than fleas, but that is a proverb which expresses smallness. Our Lord employs the mustard seed in this way. Proverbially, it is the smallest of all seeds.

Here, he is evidently stressing the apparent insignificance of the gospel. It does not look like much. It does not sound like much. When you proclaim, "Believe on the Lord Jesus Christ and you will be saved," it does not sound very impressive to many people. It is so simple that you can teach it to children. Even people who can be taught little else can understand, "Believe on the Lord Jesus Christ." So the world is not very excited about it or very much impressed with it. The world does not regard it as a tremendous, earth-shaking philosophy. You do not find chairs of philosophy in the universities dedicated to the study of the gospel in its simplicity. It is insignificant, it is despised. But let someone actually believe it and see what happens. Let him really trust Christ and invite him into his life and it is the most transforming, the most revolutionary thing that can occur to him. It is the beginning of a radical change in his whole life.

A young law student, troubled with intellectual problems about Christianity, once came to see me. As we discussed some of the intellectual barriers he was struggling with, I could sense that underneath he had a tremendous hunger. He had been impressed by the radiance and beauty of life that he had seen in a number of Christians. I soon realized that his trouble was not intellectual at all; it was simply that he thought this was the way to find God, that he had to think it all through and answer all the questions before he could become a Christian.

As well as I could, I tried to help him see that God would reach him and meet him right where he was on the basis of a venture of faith, that if he responded to the promise of God he could put God to the test. Either God would come through and fulfill his promise or he would not, one or the other, and then he would know. So this young man made the venture. He received the Lord Jesus into his heart. Simply, quietly, he asked him to come in. And almost immediately he broke into tears of relief, and a joy filled his heart. He was radiant, and said, "What a difference!" He called up a friend and the first thing he said was, "I'm a Christian! And the best thing is, Jesus keeps talking to me all the time from within." Just like that his life was transformed! That was the greatest thing that ever happened to him. Nothing will be the same again, forever. What a simple message, and yet how mighty it is! This is the seed our Lord is talking about. This message of the kingdom is like a seed of mustard with fantastic power and pungency planted in the midst of society.

NO SUCH TREE

But now look at the tree that grows out of it. Our Lord said, ". . . but when it has grown it is the greatest of shrubs and becomes a tree, so that the birds of the air come and make nests in its branches" (Matt. 13:32). Now here is the key to this parable. Did you ever see a mustard tree? In California we have fields of mustard every spring. You can see acres of the yellow flowers. But none of them ever grows into a tree; mustard is not a tree. It is an annual that dies every year. It is impossible for it to grow into a tree.

When I was in Israel a number of years ago, I was taken out by the side of the Sea of Galilee and shown a "mustard tree." It was a small tree about ten or twelve feet high with a little berry on it which the guide opened and showed us was filled with a black powder which he called mustard seed. The grains were very tiny, and he said that this is what Jesus meant—

the smallest of all seeds. I still have some of this powder in my desk. But I checked up on it later and found out that it isn't a seed at all; it is just black powder, and it will never grow into a tree. And that wasn't a mustard tree, either. It was another kind of tree. But the tourist agency has come up with something which matches this parable, and they have labelled it a mustard tree. (One of the things you learn in touring Israel is to take everything with a heavy dose of salt.)

No, mustard is not a tree; it does not grow into a tree. Then why did Jesus say it did? Right there is the heart of the parable. Our Lord obviously intended to teach that this growth is unnatural growth. It is not normal, not what you would expect from mustard seed. It is something different than is to be expected. He is surely teaching that in this age there is to be an unnatural, unusual growth. Instead of the lowly, humble plant you would expect from a mustard seed there would be a huge, abnormal, ungainly growth into a tree.

What is the meaning of that? Well, what is the normal result that you expect when the gospel comes into a human heart? What kind of character does it produce? From the Scriptures and from experience we know that it produces lowliness of heart. It takes away pride, destroys egotism and self-centeredness and renders a person humble and lowly of mind, meek and gentle toward others, ready to serve. Jesus said, "He that is greatest in the kingdom of heaven must become the least of all. If any would become great among

you, let him become the servant of all" (Mark 9:35).
That is the normal, natural, usual result of the mustard seed's growth. So what would unnatural growth
be? It would be loftiness, pride, ambition, domination
of others, concern for self. That is unnatural growth
from this kind of seed.

When a tree is used symbolically in Scripture, it
always stands for authority and power and dominion.
In the Book of Daniel, Nebuchadnezzar is symbolized
by a tree. Pharaoh, in Exodus, is symbolized by a tree.
These were men of power and authority. And what do
we find has happened in the world in these last twenty
centuries? Christendom, which began to spread among
men in the simplicity recounted in the Book of Acts
—like a humble, lowly plant, but pungent and biting
in its effects—has grown into a huge, ungainly, abnormal tree, concerned with power and pride and
domination, wanting to be served instead of to serve.
Isn't that true? Probably the blackest day in the history of the Christian church was that day in the fourth
century when the emperor Constantine made Christianity the state religion of the Roman empire and
elevated the church to a position of worldly power
from whence it went on to claim rule even over em-
perors and to dictate terms to kings—the false greatness of external position and power which became like
a great tree in the midst of society.

Protestants tend to say that applies to the Roman
Catholic Church, but it isn't the Catholic Church
alone that has experienced unnatural growth. That
church has its elements of both the pungency of the

true mustard seed and an unnatural growth into a great tree of towering pomposity and power, but so has Protestantism. We are just as guilty. We have built our great, imposing church buildings and even in evangelical circles have been concerned with our prestige, our status in the community, and our image and have sought the patronage and the admiration of the world. We have advertised ourselves, have found every way that we can to publicize ourselves and keep ourselves before the eyes of the world.

THE CHURCH DOESN'T SAVE ANYBODY

But God never intended the church to do that. The church, as Paul says in Ephesians 4, is to come with lowliness and gentleness and meekness of character, not talking about itself. The early Christians never went around talking about the church. In the Book of Acts you never see a word about the church as part of the proclamation of the gospel. The church doesn't save anybody; the Lord does. The church doesn't help anyone; it is the Lord who helps. Wherever these early Christians went they never mentioned the church until after a person joined the family of God. They talked about the Lord.

A number of years ago I heard a story about Dr. Osward J. Smith, the great missionary preacher from Toronto. He was in Brazil and was being shown through one of the great Protestant cathedrals there. It was a very impressive building with high Gothic arches and beautiful stained-glass windows—very expensive. He went through in silence, never saying a word, because his concern, his heartbeat, had always been for missions. When they finished the tour, he said to the guide, "How many missionaries does this church support?" The guide was nonplussed and said, "I'm sorry, Sir, I don't know. I'll ask the pastor. He's standing right here." And the pastor said, "Well, we have two missionaries." Dr. Smith looked around at this expensive building and said, "You support *two* missionaries? This church is a stench in the nostrils of God!" I don't know what kind of hit that made with the pastor, but it does point up the very thing our Lord is getting at here.

And you know, we can find the same tendency in our own attitudes. We are sometimes not content to be humble and little-known—busy proclaiming the burning, pungent message of Christ. We often crave a degree of prominence and position. Like James and John we covet a position at the right hand of the Lord. We want to be seen and known and admired of men. But when we are quite content not to say a word about the church we belong to, we have a wide-open door of opportunity and service by which to magnify the Lord Jesus. When we maintain a low profile in the community, there is almost nothing we can't do. But the minute we begin to attract some notoriety and publicity, then our influence begins to ebb. This is right in line with what our Lord has said.

Notice also that this tree was to have many great branches. We are not pressing the symbol too far to see this as a prediction of the many divisions and denominations of Christendom. In each town or community to which they went the apostles always organized churches which were independent of one another governmentally but were united together in the love and fellowship of the Spirit. They were bound together by mutual interests, but never organizationally. But eventually human wisdom began to intervene and these separate groups were incorporated into associations, and in comparatively recent times great divisions and denominational distinctions of Christendom have emerged. How like a tree they are. And yet, despite this abnormal growth we must remember that the seed our Lord planted was *his* seed and the mustard nature is still present even though it is obscured and difficult to see behind the towering pride and elevated position of much of the great tree.

NESTS FOR VULTURES

Finally, what is the significance of the birds which come and make their nests in the branches? We do not have to look very far for the understanding of that. Right in this very series of parables our Lord tells us what the birds mean. In the first parable he said that when the seed of the Word falls upon a hardened human heart, the birds come and snatch it away. And in his interpretation he said that the birds represented the evil one, the enemy, whose evil powers and forces are at work upon men's lives.

If the Lord had not said that, we might have read a different meaning into this parable. There is an interpretation of this parable which says that this is a picture of the gospel going out to all the world and growing up into an impressive church and that the birds are songbirds—robins and bluebirds and others which come and make their nests, which are symbols of beautiful things which happen in the church. But that would be exactly opposite to the way our Lord uses this symbol. These are not songbirds; they are vultures and buzzards, birds of prey—apt symbols of evil persons and evil ideas which make their home right in God's church.

This is confirmed in the Book of Revelation. The false church is symbolized there by the great harlot and the mystery city called "Babylon the Great." When it is overthrown, an angel announces that "Babylon the Great is fallen, and has become the habitation of demons, and the haunt of every foul spirit, and of every unclean and hateful bird" (Rev. 18:2).

How visibly this has been demonstrated in our day when from the pulpits and the spokesmen of the church has come a flood of stupid, crazy, mixed-up ideas— evil concepts which have blasted and blighted and ruined the hearts and minds of people, just as our Lord said. These things have only occurred since the tree has become fully grown and branched out, as we near the end of the age. It was only a comparatively short time ago that the great denominations of our day, though they represented unnatural and abnormal development, still were basically true to the faith and stood solidly on the authority of the Bible and proclaimed a true gospel. But then along came German rationalization and higher critical theories and socialistic philosophies. The Bible was overthrown. Another gospel was substituted and supernatural faith was denied; in many places the birds of prey moved right into the pulpits. One by one men of true faith were driven out. And it is still happening today. No wonder that when the youth of today look at the part of the church which is like that they say, "It is strictly for the birds!"

But what a comfort it is that our Lord had no delusions about this age! How clearly he foresaw all that has happened. How precisely he unfolds it to us here so we might not be deluded either. How shall we apply this to our lives? Well, obviously, it is important that we retain the nature of the mustard seed, that we be fiery and active and pungent and burning, without doing anything to abet the unnatural growth of this mustard tree. We are to seek to be low-profile wherever we work, not calling attention to ourselves, not seeking to publicize and aggrandize ourselves, but to open our hearts to God and let him take care of the rest.

We are to permit nothing in our individual lives of loftiness and pride and ambition and desire for prominence and power and position within the church. We must not struggle and be rivals to one another. Where that is evidenced it always means that people do not yet understand how the church operates, because there is no need for rivalry in the church of Jesus Christ. Everyone has his own gift and his own ministry, and in fulfilling it he is always to work in cooperation with everyone else. We are called to have faith like a grain of mustard seed, our Lord said in another place, that will grow and increase in pungency and power and impact until it completely stirs up a community, arouses it, awakens it, makes it realize what is happening, and heals it.

One of these days, the Scripture says, our Lord is going to say to this great, ungainly tree, this unnatural growth, "Be thou rooted up and cast into the midst of the sea," and it shall be done. But in the meantime, we must search our own hearts to see how much of this unnatural growth is present in us, even as Christians. How much are we reflecting that which is false and unnatural, rather than that which is true and right? How much do we embody that wonderful quality of mustard which cannot be ignored, which always stirs anyone with whom we come in contact, yet which does not seek to grow into position and prominence?

Our Father, we ask you to make clear to us what is in our own lives and hearts. You who are truth, you who are light, reveal to us who we are and what we are. Help us to be honest and faithful and to know that you have already dealt with the problems in our lives. If we will but admit them and confess them and forsake them we can enter into the value of your forgiveness and your love, and go on where we ought to go. In Jesus' name, Amen.

5

The Case of the
Sneaky Housewife

The fourth parable which Jesus used to continue his one-day marathon of teaching about the kingdom of heaven is contained in a single verse:

> He told them another parable. "The kingdom of heaven is like leaven which a woman took and hid in three measures of meal, till it was all leavened" (Matt. 13:33).

I have entitled this study "The Case of the Sneaky Housewife," not because I am trying for a tricky title but because that undoubtedly reflects the reaction of the disciples when they heard this little story. Our Lord brought them up short and shocked them somewhat with this parable. When he told them that there was a woman who hid leaven in three measures of meal, they must immediately have thought, "What a dirty trick! What a sneaky thing to do!" If it does not strike us that way, it is because we are not in their shoes. We do not understand the symbols as Jesus used them. So again, we must put ourselves back in their place and hear this story as they heard it.

This is one of those parables which has been greatly misinterpreted. Its meaning has been grossly distorted into something entirely different from what our Lord intended. Most of the major commentators on this passage seem to throw all principles of interpretation to the winds to take no notice of how Scripture uses these symbols in other places. So they arrive at a meaning which is simply a result of their own wishful thinking.

POPULAR AND WRONG

The usual interpretation is that the leaven is the gospel and the woman is the church. The church is to take the gospel and put it into the world of humanity, which is represented by the three measures of meal. The gospel quietly but surely will work away like leaven, like yeast in bread, until all of humanity is reached by the gospel and the whole world is changed. Then, finally, the kingdom of heaven will come in. Though that is far and away the most popular interpretation of this parable it is absolutely wrong! On the basis of that interpretation men have thought at various times and places that the church was going to introduce the millennium to the world, that it would bring in the kingdom, that the gospel would so permeate the affairs and the thinking of men that the outlook and insights and moral standards of Christianity would be universally accepted all over the world.

This was the fundamental philosophy of the time around the turn of this century. Men actually thought that we were right on the verge of the Golden Age. This was back in the days when William Jennings Bryan was the great spokesman for Christendom in the United States. Under his leadership many people of that time wore little golden plowshares in their lapels to symbolize the hope that this was the day in which men would beat their swords into plowshares and their spears into pruninghooks and would learn war no more.

The twentieth century began with this note of tremendous optimism. The thinking was that Christian teaching had so permeated life that we no longer would have strife between capital and labor, there no longer would be any poverty or violence among mankind, and that surely wars had been brought to an end. And this interpretation of this parable was widely proclaimed as proof that our Lord had said this would come about. The church would transform the world and put an end to war and strife and injustice and all such terrible things among men. That kind of interpretation sounds almost ludicrous to us today. Yet I can remember, as a boy growing up in the twenties and thirties that this was still very much the thought of the hour even after World War I had brought its terrible devastation.

But if I were convinced that this is the true meaning of this parable, I would be greatly tempted to throw away my Bible and give up the ministry. If this is the correct interpretation, then Jesus Christ was mistaken. For here we are, two thousand years after our Lord told this story, and there are outstanding, increasingly significant signs, from day to day almost, which indicate that we are nearing the time which our Lord at the end of this series of parables called the "close of the age." If that is the correct interpretation, then we should see the world almost completely leavened by the gospel, almost entirely Christian.

But what are the actual facts. Well, you know as well as I that never in all of history has there been more hatred, more crime, more violence, more injustice, more wretchedness, more vicious evil, among mankind than there is in our day. Of all the centuries, historians agree, the twentieth is the bloodiest. There has been more persecution of Christians in the twentieth century than ever before, including the first century. The world is a hundred times more pagan today than it was in the days of the Apostle Paul. In fifty years a godless, materialistic philosophy called communism has grown from just a handful of men to spread over half the earth. More than a billion people are under the control of this completely atheistic system. Even in our own so-called Christian country a poll taken not long ago rated the birth of Christ fourteenth in a list of important events in history. Though more Bibles are being sold than ever before, still fifty percent of the people of this country cannot name even one of the Gospels. Either Christ has failed or something has gone desperately wrong with his program if the common interpretation of this parable is to be accepted.

But if we will listen and react to this story as that crowd did, we will recognize the true interpretation of this parable. Our Lord did not interpret this parable to his disciples because he evidently expected them to know what the meaning was. In fact, a little later, when they were in the house, he asked them if they knew what these parables meant and they said they did.

Jesus is using here a very common picture from any Hebrew household, and everyone present knew he meant that this woman was doing an evil, sneaky thing when she hid this leaven in the meal. So we want to look at this as they would have with their background and their understanding of what these symbols mean. Let's begin with the meal. It is the central element in this story. The woman and the leaven both did something to the three measures of meal. That is what our Lord is trying to get across to us. So the central question is: "What does the meal represent?"

THE MEAL OFFERING

This crowd of Jews would know instantly what he had in mind. With their Judaistic background and training in the Old Testament their minds would flash back immediately to one of the most common offerings in Israel—the meal offering, consisting of three measures of meal carefully prescribed to be unleavened, without any yeast in it at all.

Very likely many of them would think back to the

very first time the phrase "three measures of meal" appears in the Scriptures. It is in Genesis 18. Abraham was in his tent by the oaks of Mamre one day, and he looked out the door and saw three strangers approaching. He went to meet them, for strangers were an uncommon sight in those days and anyone passing by was offered hospitality. He welcomed them and offered them three measures of meal which Sarah baked into bread while they were visiting together out under the trees. During their conversation it suddenly broke upon Abraham's astonished intelligence that God himself was visiting him, accompanied by two angels. That was the beginning of the use of the three measures of meal as a symbol.

What did it mean? It is clear that it became a symbol of the fellowship of God with his people and their fellowship with one another. Meal is a beautiful picture of commonality of life. In the Bible it is always a picture of humanity, a humanity which is all alike. Just as each grain of cereal or meal is like all the other grains, people are alike and share in the same quality and nature. And they blend together to make up something valuable. So, very early in the life of the Jewish people the three measures of meal became a picture of the people of God sharing the life and the fellowship of God. When the Old Testament people offered the three measures of meal, they were describing in beautifully picturesque language what was very precious in God's sight—the oneness of God with his family, God with his people, the life they shared with each other under the Fatherhood of God.

Later on, in the Book of Judges, when Gideon was suddenly confronted with the angel of God, he brought him an offering of three measures of unleavened meal. When Hannah, the mother of Samuel, went to worship God in the temple she took with her an offering of three measures of meal, unleavened. So this is a common symbol throughout the Old Testament, and it was familiar to these Jews to whom Jesus spoke. They knew instantly what he meant.

In 1 Corinthians, Paul said to the church at Corinth that the key thing about their lives as Christians was that they were called into the fellowship of God: "God is faithful, by whom you were called into the fellowship of his Son, Jesus Christ our Lord" (1 Cor. 1:9). This is the key to that great letter. That is what Christianity is all about. It is the sharing of the life of Jesus together. We share his life and all that he is. And when John opens his first letter he says,

> . . . that which we have seen and heard we proclaim also to you, so that you may have fellowship with us; and our fellowship is with the Father and with his Son Jesus Christ (1 John 1:3).

So there is the meaning of the three measures of meal, the unleavened bread of sincerity, honesty, and truth. It is very precious to God that his people become honest and open and acceptant toward one another, with nothing hidden between them. They are to understand one another, bear one another's burdens, uphold one another, and share together the life of God in their midst, the life of a living Lord. That is what our Lord introduced into the world by bringing the gospel—this marvelous seed dropped into the heart of humanity which produces a willingness to be open and to stop hiding behind facades and to be honest in sharing the forgiving grace of Jesus Christ.

SYMBOL OF EVIL

Now let's look at the leaven. The disciples would quickly recognize its meaning. It is used all through the Old Testament, and always the same way. Never once is leaven used as a symbol of anything good. Everyone in this crowd knew that this woman had no business putting leaven into the three measures of meal. That would destroy the very meaning of this significant offering, for Scripture had taught them that the three measures of meal were to be unleavened. You remember that in Egypt, before the Jews ate the first Passover, God sent them all through their houses with candles and lamps looking for leaven. They were to clear every bit of it out of the house lest any of it get into the three measures of meal for the Passover feast and destroy the beauty of the symbolism. They were to search meticulously, to look in corners, on shelves, and in the closets. (Perhaps this is where the custom of spring house cleaning began because Passover is in the spring.) The Jewish people still do this today as a result of that teaching way back in the time of Moses.

In the New Testament you find five distinct references to leaven, and they all mean something bad. Never, ever in the Scriptures does leaven symbolize something good; it is always a type of something evil.

Jesus frequently spoke of leaven. He said to his disciples, "Beware of the leaven of the Pharisees." And, lest we misunderstand what he meant, Luke adds: "The leaven of the Pharisees is hypocrisy," pretending to be something you are not, pretending to a status before God which you don't actually possess, being phony, putting on an outward appearance of religiosity but inwardly still having the same old evil thoughts and angry moods and bitter attitudes. That is the leaven of the Pharisees—hypocrisy.

Then Jesus spoke of the leaven of the Sadducees. That is rationalism—the idea that life consists only of what you can taste and see and touch and smell and hear and think about, that there is nothing beyond that, no supernatural activity of God in life, no resurrection, no angels, no life after death.

And he spoke of the leaven of the Herodians, the followers of King Herod. Their leaven was materialism. They taught that the great value of life is to be powerful and wealthy. If you can acquire wealth and power, then you have the secret of life. Many today are following the philosophy of the Herodians, holding the attitude that what makes life worthwhile is the possession of things. That is evil, Jesus says. That is not the way you properly measure manhood or the value of a life.

In his Epistles the Apostle Paul spoke of leaven. In 1 Corinthians 5 he cites the case of a man who was actually living in incest with his father's wife, and Paul says that sexual immorality is leaven within the church, destroying its fellowship. He goes on to say,

Your boasting is not good. Do you not know that a little leaven leavens [ferments] the whole lump [of dough]? Cleanse out the old leaven that you may be a new lump [fresh dough], as you really are unleavened. For Christ, our paschal lamb, has been sacrificed. Let us, therefore, celebrate the festival, not with the old leaven, the leaven of malice and evil, but with the unleavened bread of sincerity and truth (1 Cor. 5:6–8).

That is what the bread stood for: sincerity, honesty, truth, and openness—a recognition of each other's value and a transparency before each other. Anything which wrecks or ruins that or distorts it and puffs it up is leaven.

Finally, in the Book of Galatians Paul again speaks of leaven, this time in connection with legalism. There were false teachers who tried to put people under the law, under a set of rules by which to live, expecting them to have the power to obey simply by their own effort. The very heart of the gospel is that Christ has come to set us free from that. The world has been trying to live on that basis for centuries, and it has never been successful. Every effort to obey a rule and thus to satisfy God even with external obedience, let alone internal, is doomed to failure before it begins if you are depending upon yourself for the necessary power. That way of life is called leaven. It, too, destroys the fellowship of God's people.

So leaven, obviously, is anything which disintegrates, breaks up, and corrupts, or causes a puffed up, swollen condition—destroying honesty and obscuring reality. That is what yeast does when you put it into bread. The housewife says that it lightens the bread because it puffs it up, swells it up. At a certain point she arrests the action of the yeast by baking the bread in the oven. But leavened bread will spoil far more quickly than unleavened. Leaven is disruptive and corrupting.

WHODUNNIT?

Now we come to the last symbol and the key question. Here we have these two elements: (1) the fellowship of God's people which, as Jesus looked down the age, he saw as a very precious and important way of life which he had introduced into society, and (2) something which corrupts that by introducing this five-fold evil of leaven into the fellowship. Who does this? Who is this woman? The French, you know, have a little saying they use whenever trouble arises: "Cherchez la femme," "look for the woman." I don't know but what this may be the origin of that saying.

Some of the commentators have tried to identify the woman in this parable with a specific woman in history, and it is amazing what they have come up with. Some suggest it is Joan of Arc, who is supposed to have destroyed the fellowship of the church by introducing false doctrines. Others have said, no, it is Mary Baker Eddy, the founder of Christian Science. And I remember meeting some people back in the forties who identified her with Eleanor Roosevelt, of all people. It may be that some today are tempted to say that it is the Women's Liberation Movement that is introducing these evils.

But when a woman is used symbolically in Scripture it always means the same thing—some religious authority either out of place or doing the wrong thing, some misuse of a relationship with God. It is clear that the woman belongs in the story. A woman is an authority in the home, one who had the right to prepare the bread of fellowship. This woman was in her rightful place, in her kitchen. It was her job to prepare the bread. But she had no right to hide leaven in it. And the very fact that she hides it indicates sneaky motives; she is trying to get away with something she knows is wrong.

Now bring the picture together. Our Lord is looking down the centuries to follow and he sees the thing which is most precious to God about the work which he himself has begun among mankind. This is the fellowship of God with his people, the sharing of life with each other and with God, the family of God, the oneness of the body of Christ—with all the members sharing life in openness and honesty together under the love and forgiveness of the Father. And into that wonderful fellowship these false, evil principles are introduced by those who had the right and the authority to preserve this fellowship, that is, the leaders of the church. It is they who introduce the leaven into it, who permit it to come in and do not exclude it as they should. Those who are charged with the responsibility of developing the fellowship of God's people, nevertheless, allow hypocrisy, formalism, ritualism, rationalism, materialism, legalism, immorality—all of these things—to come in. And when these things get into a church, they destroy the fellowship of God's people.

What an instructive parable this is! As we apply it to ourselves, we can see that this is what has been happening. This is why churches are often charged with being cold and unfriendly—there's no fellowship. It is too often only on the most superficial basis that people come and sit together in the congregation. They come, not as members together of one great family, but as individuals—listening to the service, but not relating to the person next to them. But that isn't Christianity as it is intended to be manifested. That is only a form, only a moment in the Christian life. The major part is to be the sharing of each other's concerns, the bearing of one another's burdens, the confessing of our faults one to another and praying for one another that we may be healed, the opening of our lives and the transparency of our actions before others. This is the great fellowship that our Lord is seeking.

As you trace this pattern down through history, you can see how leaven has been working. The very ones who were responsible to keep God's house free from it—the leaders, the pastors, the elders, the teachers within the church—are the ones responsible for allowing these conditions to come in and prevail. And each time they have done so they have destroyed this marvelous fellowship.

THE MOST PRECIOUS THING

Now, openness and oneness of the body together is the key to all revival. Every time the Spirit of God has ever moved in history he has always begun here. He has restored to the church the sense of belonging to each other and to God together, the sense of openness and honesty and transparency. He has also restored the sense of the need to bear each other's burdens and to uphold one another before God, to be concerned and to care for each other, and to demonstrate it by deeds of help and mercy toward each other—all because we share the life of God. We are free to do this because we do not have to be hung up with defensiveness about ourselves. We have received the forgiveness of God, the grace of God, and that frees us to be at one with someone else. This is the most precious thing in the world in God's sight. It is that three measures of meal which marks a humanity undivided, a humanity which belongs to each other.

You see in the early church this evident oneness. This is the emphasis of the Book of Acts. Notice how warm and sweet and precious is the fellowship together of the people of God in that book. We read, "They had all things in common," and the word "common" is the very word for fellowship. It was not that they pooled all their property, like the communists, and doled it out to each other. That isn't the idea. It means that in owning private property they recognized the claim of their brothers and sisters upon it, as well as themselves, and that if God gave them something, he gave it to be used for all. They were, therefore, generous and open with each other. Since they recognized that they all belonged to one family, anybody who was in need could ask of anyone else and that

need would be met. This is the level of life on which
they lived. You find this all through the Book of Acts
and the result was that "they had great power in wit-
nessing, and great grace was upon them all."

That is what is often lacking in the church today.
We have taken away the "koinonia," the commonness
of the body of Christ. We have lost that to a great
extent in the church in general. But we have held onto
the "kerygma," the preaching, the proclamation. We
expect to convince everybody by an intellectual pres-
entation of truth. But the reason the evangelical church
of our day is rejected and set aside in so many quarters
is that people who come to it are disappointed because they hear great words but they don't see great
lives—they don't see warmth, love, acceptance, understanding, forgiveness. What they too often run into is
strife and bickering and fighting and quarreling and
unforgiveness. They see jealousy and bitterness,
grudges and splits and feuds and divisions, hostility
and anger, worry and anxiety. They listen to the
preaching of these great words which the church has
to say and then they look at our lives to see how it
works. And what they see convinces them that the
words are not true.

What they see is exactly what they find in their own
lives and homes. So they say to us, "What are you
Christians talking about? What's the difference? What
do you Christians have that we don't have—without
the inconvenience of having to go through all the rites
you go through. What is so great about this message?
Why doesn't it do something for you? Why should we

believe it and go to all the trouble of becoming a Christian when we can live the same way you do ourselves? We don't need the church or the Bible to teach us how to fight. We don't need the gospel to help us to be angry and resentful and bitter and divided against each other. We can do all that without it." And so there is an immediate loss of attention to the message that we are proclaiming because there is no evidence of the witness of communion. What is missing is the oneness, the precious fellowship together of the people of God living the life of God.

SPIRIT OF FORMALISM

Our Lord knew this would happen. He knew that leaven would appear within the church, allowed there by those who had the authority to keep it out if only they would. First there came the leaven of the Pharisees—hypocrisy. The Pharisees said that you please God when everything involving the externals of your life is right. When you watch your language so that you don't use blasphemous words and pay all your debts and keep up your church attendance, then everything is all right. Your heart can be filled with all kinds of bitterness and hatred and enmity and lust and fear, but as long as you maintain outward appearances, you are acceptable before God. That is a deadly bit of leaven, and it will destroy the warmth of the fellowship of God's people with himself and with each other. But that is what has happened so often.

In the very early days of the new church, Ananias and Sapphira, even though they were Christians, began to pretend to a degree of dedication and commitment which they really did not have. God judged it to show us what that was (Acts 5:1–11). It was leaven at work and it destroyed, it brought sudden death into their midst, as it does into our lives today the minute we try to pretend with each other·

This is what has happened to the meetings of the church. A spirit of formalism has come in. Formality is a way of making the exterior appear to be right while inwardly your heart can be whatever it happens to be at the moment. But you do not have to show it to anyone. Formality is coming into church and looking pious and dedicated and evangelical, or whatever you want to call it, while the inward state of the heart is a far cry from the external appearance. That is formalism, ritualism, and it is the leaven of hypocrisy.

I am distressed by the widespread attitude these days that the only way you can worship God properly is to be "reverent"—which means to be quiet—that it is wrong to talk when you come into a church service because a service ought to be attended in silence. I suppose nothing is more commonplace in Christianity than the idea that people should come and sit quietly before the service begins. Don't say anything to anybody, just come and sit and bow your head. Don't even look at your neighbor when he sits down or greet him in any way.

But that is a hangover from the days of the Jewish temple when the presence of God caused a spirit of great awe to settle upon the people. This was carried over into Catholic and Protestant churches, with their cold, formal architecture. People coming into church were taught that they were entering the "house of God," and that the only way to act before God is to be reserved and half-frightened. This is wrong! You don't find this among the New Testament Christians. Their practice was to come together and relate to each other *and* to God. When the body of Christ comes together, we are to recognize and love each other. God does not dwell in temples made by hands; he dwells in the bodies of believers. His life is warm, open, and acceptant. And we worship God when we enjoy fellowship with each other. I think a church is healthy when there is whispering and talking and visiting and relating one to another until the service begins.

I know there are moments in a service when we should be quiet, when everyone is quiet before God. But there is nothing irreverent about visiting with one another, relating to each other, before or even after a service begins, nothing at all! That is the way it ought to be in the presence of God. The idea that it is wrong to react in church, or to find out how people are and what they are doing and to pray with them a bit, is absolutely foreign to the New Testament concept of the church. We are to love one another and to manifest this when we come together. That which teaches the contrary is introducing the leaven of hypocrisy into the church.

SEEDS OF REBELLION

You know how rampant legalism is in the church today. Christians are trying to control themselves and

their children by law and not by grace by trying to
make a list of rules according to which people are to
live. This is absolutely destructive to the Christian
life. The idea has been that if we teach our children
what is right, that if we hold up before them a moral
code or standard complete with all the little variations
of our own (no-no's that we have added here and
there), that we have thus discharged our responsibility
as Christian parents. But that is basic and fundamental
legalism, and it will produce rebellion—as it is now
and has been producing all along.

Law is necessary, of course, in our children's lives
in order to maintain order in life and in the home,
and the Scriptures teach this. But the whole idea of
being parents is to teach children that there is another
basis on which they can react to situations. There is
the basis not of demand ("You must do this or I
will not love you") but of love ("I already love you,
and whatever you do I will love you—nothing is going
to destroy our relationship). There you have a relationship with God from which you can draw upon his
strength and his grace to respond to whatever life is
requiring of you. That is what we are parents for—to
teach them that basis.

We need to remember that as parents our responsibility is to teach our children *how* to respond to a
demand, by what power. We must teach them that
Jesus Christ, living his life within us, makes it possible
to meet these demands. We must first demonstrate this
as parents. Then we must teach it and explain it from
the Scriptures, but without the demonstration the

Scriptures will be meaningless. This is what is wrong in so many Christian homes. There is no demonstration of the way to meet the pressures of life by faith in a living Lord. You haven't taught Christianity when you have merely held up the moral standard of the Ten Commandments. You have taught Christianity only when you have shown that Jesus died for us in order that he might live in us and that his life imparted to us is the basis on which we respond to his law. Anything other than that is the leaven of legalism.

Then there is a leaven of rationalism. And how that has come into the church! Men have forgotten that the Word of God is a revelation of truth given to us by God—truth that we could never know if he had not told it to us. Therefore, it is superior to and beyond anything that is available in our universities or anything that man can find out for himself. All that contradicts a proper understanding of God's revelation must be denied.

Then there is the leaven of materialism whereby many Christians have actually succumbed to the idea that the really important things in life are to have a fine home, lovely luxuries, a swimming pool, color TV, and three or four cars. They build their lives around these things, aim at them as goals, and are distressed and disenchanted and discontented if they cannot have them. And their children pick up the idea that these are the important things in life, that status and prestige in the community and your image before your neighbors are paramount. That is the leaven of materialism and it destroys this sweet fellowship of God.

Finally, there is the leaven of immorality—and how that spreads in a church! And yet, as any honest, knowledgeable psychologist can tell you, sex practiced outside of marriage is a most dangerous and harmful way to wreck and ruin a relationship. I have had scores and scores of young people sit in my study and confirm this to me. Again and again they have told me how a beautiful relationship was developing between two people, but when they went into sex, the development was arrested at that level; they never got to know each other any more deeply than that. This is why God excludes sex outside marriage; it destroys the oneness of loving and growing together and precludes really knowing each other.

LOCKED IN

I am shocked to hear how many churches are now taking a stand in defense of homosexuality, as though this is to be accepted as a way of life. I don't think there is any more deadly thing we can do to those who are homosexuals than to take a stand like that because it locks them into a pattern of defeat from which there is no escape. The same applies to any other form of sexual deviation or misbehavior. If any of these practices are accepted as right, they will spread like leaven, destroying the fellowship and the openness of God's people one with another and with the Father. The church is to understand that those who indulge in these things are in the grip of terrible, difficult problems and that love and grace ought to reach out to them and welcome them and put an arm around their shoulder and help them in their struggle. But never, never are we to compromise and say that this is something they have to live with. They don't have to live with it. Christ has come to set us free from all forms of bondage, whether it be the bondage of legalism, of immorality, of a materialistic outlook, or whatever. Our Lord has come to set us free! That is what Christianity is all about.

We can see the results of this leaven that has come into the church on every side. But God has made provision for being cleansed from leaven. By the forgiveness of the cross, by the simple method of admitting the facts and then accepting the forgiveness of God without any further quibble, we can be washed, cleansed, and can go on together from that point as free men and women, no longer in bondage to these things but set free by the grace of God. We can then begin to be transparent and open once again.

How wise our Lord is! How accurately he sees what is happening. How quickly and honestly our Lord has put his finger upon the course of this age and shown us the very things which destroy and corrupt the sweet fellowship of the people of God. He warns us very clearly against allowing leaven to come into our fellowship. And this word is addressed especially to those in authority and leadership within the church. For the teaching of the Word of truth will arrest the action of the leaven.

If the leaders of the church through the centuries had faithfully stuck with the Scripture and had taught it as it is, these unhappy developments would have been prevented. But everywhere I go as a pastor today, speaking to groups of other pastors, I find out that this is the great weakness—pastors are not teaching the Bible. They are not instructing their people from the Word of God and teaching what it actually says about how they are to live together. They aren't saying a word about that. They are discussing remote doctrinal questions and giving their opinions on the social and political issues of the day instead of instructing in what the Bible is really aimed at—the very personal lives of individuals and their relationships one with another. If the leadership of the church were carefully going over the Scriptures together with people, unfolding the Word of God, the whole effect of leaven would be greatly minimized within the body of Christ.

Thank God for those places all over the country today where pastors have reached the end of their efforts to do it another way and are returning at last to the Word, beginning to unfold and proclaim it before the people. That is the business of preaching—to help people understand their lives in the light of the revelation of the Word of God so that together we might share openly and honestly and transparently before one another the living grace and forgiveness of our Father in heaven.

Thank you, Father, for truth that opens our eyes, that reveals to us where we are. And thank you, Lord, for the beautiful symbol of the fellowship of your people with each other and with you which you have given us in the three measures of meal. Lord Jesus, you who have come into this world to break the strange and

cold fetters which bind us away from one
another, away from the expression of love and
life together, forgive us. Grant us, Lord, that
there may be a putting away of the leaven in
order that the sweetness and beauty of your life
may be evident in our midst and that we may
love each other in the grace and forgiveness that
you have given to us. Help us to lay hold of the
healing grace of Jesus Christ our Lord and to
be cleansed and made whole in his strength, by
his grace. We ask in his name, Amen.

6

The Case

of the Buried Treasure

In the great series of parables in Matthew 13 our Lord gave us, as he said, "The secrets of the kingdom of heaven." The kingdom of heaven is God's work among men, God's rule and authority in the midst of human affairs. In this series Jesus is revealing the work of the kingdom as it is going on throughout the centuries of this present age since his first coming and before his return.

I don't know what the thought of buried treasure may evoke in your mind, but it always reminds me of Robert Louis Stevenson's *Treasure Island*, of Long John Silver, of doubloons and pieces-of-eight, of peg-leg pirates, and all the exciting things usually associated with the idea of buried treasure. It is intriguing to realize that Scripture deals with this subject as well. It recognizes the allure and the mystery which always gathers around the notion of hidden treasure. God has his buried treasures, too, and he is speaking of them in this fifth parable.

The first four parables were delivered by the sea of Galilee when Jesus spoke to the assembled people from a boat. But this parable of the treasure hidden in the field is the first of a series of three which our Lord gave to the disciples alone, as Matthew is careful to tell us, after they had gone back into the house. Although they are part of the whole series of seven, it is significant that these three were given only to the disciples.

The first four stories were given to the unbelieving seaside crowd. They concern those aspects of the kingdom of heaven at work among men which are readily recognizable and visible in history. But these last three were spoken only to the men of faith, the disciples, who were ready to believe what God said. They concern things which are not quite as easily seen in the historical process.

The parables of the hidden treasure and of the pearl of great price are twin parables. Because they are so closely linked, let's read them together, although we will look only at the first one in this chapter:

> "The kingdom of heaven is like treasure hidden in a field, which a man found and covered up; then in his joy he goes and sells all that he has and buys that field.
> "Again, the kingdom of heaven is like a merchant in search of fine pearls, who, on finding one pearl of great value, went and sold all that he had and bought it" (Matt. 13:44–46).

You can see that these parables are very much alike. They each have the element of a man who discovers something valuable and sells all that he has and buys it. They fit together but they are not talking about exactly the same thing.

As is the case with the parable of the leaven, these two parables have also been interpreted without any regard for the systematic interpretation of symbols in Scripture. The usual interpretation of these parables is that Christ is the hidden treasure and that he is the pearl of great price. And as we go through life, we are the people who some day discover him. Then it is up to us to sell all that we have, give it all up, and buy him at any cost.

But I submit to you that is false, and obviously so. *Never* anywhere in Scripture is salvation *ever* offered to us as something that we have to buy or can buy. We are absolute paupers in God's sight. We have nothing to offer him, nothing that we can give in return. Salvation is offered to us as a free gift, entirely by the grace of God. No one can ever give all that he has in order to purchase Jesus Christ because he has nothing to give in the first place. Therefore, let's not spend any more time on that misinterpretation but come right to the heart of what the story of the treasure hidden in the field really means.

Notice that there are two things in this story which are immediately recognizable from the previous parables. There is a man, and there is a field. So we already have clues as to what these mean. The man in these parables is always Jesus himself. He has previously identified himself as the central figure. And the field, he has told us, is the world—the world of humanity, the human race, all of society.

HIDDEN IN HUMANITY

With these clues that our Lord himself has given us we now have the key to the understanding of this parable. Jesus came, he says, and found a treasure hidden in humanity. Something was hidden, lost in the human race, but he uncovered it. And then he did an amazing thing. He covered it up again, buried it again. Then he went and gave all that he had and bought that field of humanity so he might possess the treasure.

Immediately we are asking, "What is this treasure?" That is what our Lord wants us to ask. One of the fascinating things about studying Scripture, especially in a series of parables, is to try to answer questions like that, to seek to fit the puzzle of the parable to the pattern of life and see how they correspond. Something is hidden in the world. It was hidden when our Lord came. He uncovered it but buried it again, and now it is hidden once more. And there it remains until our Lord's return. Now, what is it?

Well, is it not obvious that there is something lost with relation to humanity, something every human being seems to be seeking, consciously or unconsciously, something every thinking person throughout the world is searching for and longing for with an ache that is almost physical? Men have dreamed of finding it for centuries. They have erected great organizations to try to bring it about, to produce this hidden treasure. The United Nations exists for this very purpose. The communists claim that they have found it. The western democracies say that they have found it. But it is very evident that neither has found this secret. What would it be?

SECRET OF WORLD PEACE

The treasure is the secret of international peace, harmony among the nations. As our Lord indicates, it is something related to the field, to humanity. It is hidden within that human field so that Jesus had to buy the field in order to get the treasure. That treasure is the lost secret of how to get along with other nations, how to discover peace and prosperity and happiness and all the many benefits of peace that men have been seeking after for centuries.

Some time ago, in addressing a crowd of 2500 delegates from fifty-seven countries of the world who were trying to find some way to world peace, Secretary General of the United Nations, U Thant, said these remarkable words:

> What element is lacking so that with all our skill and all our knowledge we still find ourselves in the dark valley of discord and enmity? What is it that inhibits us from going forward together to enjoy the fruits of human endeavor and to reap the harvest of human experience? Why is it that for all our professed ideals, our hopes, and our skills, peace on earth is still a distant objective seen only dimly through the storms and turmoils of our present difficulties?

There is an honest cry from the harassed heart of a statesman who is desperately trying to find the treasure that is hidden in man, the secret of world peace.

If you want to put that treasure into one word, as revealed by the Scriptures, that word is Israel, the nation of Israel. I am sure that these disciples understood this because they were Jews themselves, and they knew their people's history and what the Old Testament revealed about them. These were men of the Word, and when our Lord spoke this parable, they would clearly remember the words of Exodus 19. God, speaking to this nation to which he has given the Law, says,

> Now therefore, if ye will obey my voice indeed, and keep my covenant, then ye shall be a peculiar treasure unto me above all people . . . (Exod. 19:5, AV).

And they would remember the words of Psalm 135:4:

> For the Lord hath chosen Jacob [another name for Israel] unto himself . . . for his peculiar treasure (AV).

A WORKING MODEL

You need only read the Book of Deuteronomy to know that God set aside this people, the Jews, in order that they should be a showcase of theocracy to all the other nations of the world. We speak of the Jews as "the chosen people," and, unfortunately, a very grave misconception of that phrase has arisen. Even the Jewish people themselves misunderstand it to a large degree. Usually people take it to mean that God has chosen the Jews for a special destiny, that they are to have special and uniquely privileged treatment different than any other nation enjoys. But such is not the case. God did not choose Israel for that purpose. He chose them to be a representative nation, to be a working model of what a nation ought to be, in order that all other nations might share that knowledge. He set them out as a sample, an example nation, to indicate by visible demonstration what God wants to be and to do with all the other nations of the world. Israel, therefore, is not a unique, select people but, rather, a people chosen to demonstrate the kind of relationship that God wants to have with every other people on earth. They are intended to demonstrate how any nation can be blessed and fulfilled and find prosperity and peace and harmony and happiness if they discover the secret of their relationship to God.

That is Israel's purpose and there was a time in their developing history when it was partially fulfilled. In the days of David and Solomon there was a demonstration to the world of their day of what God would do with a nation which was in right relationship with him. It was a partial demonstration, never complete, never full. But even that partial realization was a magnificent model of what God could do with any nation. In the days of David, and especially in those of Solomon who followed, the world beat a path to Israel to see what God was doing.

You remember the story of the Queen of Sheba who, as Jesus had said earlier this very day, came "from the ends of the earth" because she had heard of Solomon's glory, and she wanted to find the secret of this man's prestige and power and wisdom and majesty. She was no inconsiderable monarch herself. She wasn't just Queen for a Day. She was a great queen in her own right. And she brought with her a great retinue bearing exotic spices, gold, silver, precious stones, beautiful cloth—an amazing array of presents for King Solomon. These were the best she had to offer. But when King Solomon met her, he began to give presents to her, and his outweighed hers by far. She reviewed all the glories of the kingdom of Solomon and was amazed and staggered by what she saw. Then she asked him for the secret, and Solomon took her to the temple and there he showed her the worship of Jehovah—he showed her how this nation was related to the God of glory and that it was their understanding of God which produced the magnificence she had seen. The queen's heart melted, and she said, "I didn't believe the reports until I had seen all this with my own eyes, but the half was not told me!" (1 Kings 10:1–10).

Now that is God's plan for the nations—to provide a working model in the nation Israel. This is what we human beings need. We never can understand anything until we see it demonstrated before us. That is why it is not enough to preach the gospel to people; you must also live it. It is not enough to mouth great words like love and joy and peace and forgiveness; you also have to demonstrate them or people will never believe the gospel, never accept it, never receive it.

So the secret of world peace is wrapped up, bound up, in the strange nation of Israel. Only when Israel comes again into its right relationship to God will it ever be possible to have world peace. I want to make it clear that it is right that we should pursue peace. Nations are right to try to solve their problems and reconcile their differences. There is nothing wrong with that at all. But, nevertheless, the Scriptures tell us that the secret is hidden from men until it is revealed through Israel.

When our Lord came into the world and to Israel, he found that this treasure had been lost to the world. For more than four hundred years Israel had been an obscure, little nation. There was no voice of God in their midst, no prophet speaking forth from God. The nation's glory was gone. It was now subject to the Romans, crushed under the heel of an iron-hearted oppressor. Our Lord found the nation in bondage, the temple overrun with moneychangers, commercial charlatans making a fast buck by preying upon the worship of the people. He found poverty and misery stalking the land.

BRIEFLY REVEALED

When he found it, what did he do? He uncovered it. That is the story of the Gospels. He revealed for a brief flash of time the glory that was Israel. He declared it in great messages like the Sermon on the Mount. And then he demonstrated it by healing the multitudes, by driving the moneychangers out of the temple, by feeding the thousands with bread and fish, and by rebuking death and evil everywhere he went.

In the short course of the three and a half years of our Lord's ministry he uncovered the treasure of Israel, the secret of this nation's life.

But you know what happened. The nation would not have it, would not have *him,* and they rejected him. So, according to the parable, he hid the treasure again. You cannot read the Gospel stories without seeing that there came a time in our Lord's ministry when he began to change his message and turn away from the proclamation that the kingdom of heaven was at hand, that he was there in their midst. As opposition began to mount against him and resistance to his message increased, our Lord withdrew from Jerusalem and went out into the desert. He refused to go into the capital city again until his appointed hour had come. And the crowds who had followed him, the multitudes who had hung upon his words faded away. "Many turned back," the record says, "and no longer walked with him" (John 6:66).

Eventually, he came again into the city, and there he pronounced solemn and serious words of judgment against the nation. You can read them in Matthew 23 in the sharp series of woes that he pronounced against the Pharisees and the scribes. "Woe to you, scribes and Pharisees, hypocrites!" he said. Earlier he had pronounced judgment on the outlying cities: "Woe to you, Chorazin! Woe to you, Bethsaida! for if the miracles done in you had been done in Tyre and Sidon [which were pagan communities], they would have repented long ago. But you have refused."

Jesus had entered Jerusalem in what we call the triumphal entry. He would never have called it that. He went into the city riding upon an ass in fulfillment of the prophecy of Zechariah, "Behold, your king is coming to you, humble, and mounted on an ass, and on a colt, the foal of an ass" (Matt. 21:5). Instead of being received by the rulers and leaders of the people, he was rejected. A crowd of children and humble folk were the only ones who recognized him and went ahead of him waving palm branches and crying, "Hosanna! Blessed is he who comes in the name of the Lord!" He lamented over this recalcitrant city and said, "O Jerusalem, Jerusalem, killing the prophets and stoning those who are sent to you! How often would I have gathered your children together as a hen gathers her brood under her wings, and you would not! Behold, your house is forsaken and desolate. For I tell you, you will not see me again, until you say, 'Blessed is he who comes in the name of the Lord' " (Matt. 23:37–39).

Then our Lord went into the temple and he stopped the sacrifices. He ended them, and later he said to the people, "The kingdom of God will be taken away from you and given to a nation producing the fruits of it" (Matt. 21:43). By that he indicated that the privilege of demonstrating the grace of God would be taken from Israel and given to the church. The church would thereafter demonstrate before men the healing grace of God as we will see in our next study. Finally, Jesus left the city once more and went out to his death.

ALL THAT HE HAD

But the wonderful thing the Lord tells us here is that he has not given up his purpose. God has not forgotten Israel. In this little parable he reveals that he came and found this treasure, the secret of world peace and prosperity, hidden in this nation. They had lost the secret of their own lives, so he unfolded it and unveiled it for them. Then, when he was rejected by the people, he covered it over once more. But then the parable says, "Then in his joy the man went and gave all that he had and bought the field." And in those words, "he gave all that he had," the mystery of the darkness of the cross of Jesus Christ is implied. They bring to mind the words of Philippians 2: ". . . though he was in the form of God, did not count equality with God a thing to be grasped, but emptied himself [disenfranchised himself, pauperized himself —he gave all that he had] . . . and became obedient unto death, even death on a cross" (Phil. 2:6–8).

One element of what Jesus accomplished by dying on the cross was to purchase the right to set Israel again among the nations as a model so that the world might learn how to live in peace. And in that we can see revealed the heart of God who looks at this broken and fragmented world, with all its injustice, heartache, sorrow, violence, and slaughter, and yet has not forgotten his purposes and has preserved the secret of world peace in a treasure hidden among the nations—which he will someday bring forth again.

It is all too sadly evident how divided among themselves the Israelis are now and how they are separating into squabbling, bickering groups—fighting each other, with many political parties vying for power. Ringed by enemies armed to the teeth who vow to wipe every Jew off the face of the earth, the Jews obviously do not understand the secret of their own life and are trying to produce peace and stability by democratic methods and consensus and compromise. They have not yet regained the lost secret of their nation—that any nation which walks in right relationship to God, he will heal.

I have never forgotten something I learned years ago when I was in Hawaii. The motto of that fiftieth state is a result of the work of the early Christian missionaries who came from New England in the nineteenth century. It is: "Ua mau ke ea o ka aina ika pono," which means, "The life of the land is preserved by righteousness." You and I are making a great mistake if, as Americans, we think that this country is being held together by the Constitution of the United States or by the Declaration of Independence. Thank God for those documents, but they have no power to hold us together as a people, to preserve our national liberties or our national life. The life of this land, like that of every other land, is preserved by righteousness. That means obedience to God. That means a recognition of his healing power and of the fact that his forgiveness is available for all the injuries and mistakes and wrongdoings of our past. That means a change of mind, repentance, turning again to God and recognizing his presence in our midst. That is what keeps a nation strong. If our country forgets that, it will lose its ability to stand as a nation among the other nations of the world.

But the nations of earth will never learn this righteousness, finally, until Israel stands once again as a nation before God, recognizing the presence of God in their midst and providing a working model of how every nation ultimately is to be run by the provision and power of God. This parable tells us that. Our Lord came and bought the whole field so that someday he might use the treasure hidden in it to make the world blossom with glory.

A PROMISED INHERITANCE

This is what Paul tells us in the ninth, tenth, and eleventh chapters of Romans. You will never understand what God is doing in history unless you understand those three chapters. There God's relationship with this strange and wonderful people, Israel, is made clear. There, too, Paul tells us that God is not through with Israel. He has only hidden them away again. For 1900 years Israel was utterly lost among the nations, dispersed. When our Lord covered the treasure over, it was hidden completely in the field of humanity again. But in our own time we have seen an amazing wonder: one of the most remarkable things that has ever taken place in the annals of men and one of the most dramatic demonstrations of the truth of the Word of God! God has gathered this nation together again, brought in the people from the outlying countries of the world, gathered his dispersed from the four corners of the earth, and brought them back into the land. There they stand ready, being prepared right now to discover again, finally, the secret of their life. They have not found it yet, but when they do, Paul tells us, they will cause the earth to blossom and the world will move into its promised inheritance. In Romans 11, Paul says of Israel,

> So I ask, have they stumbled so as to fall? [That is, Israel had obviously stumbled at that time, but have they fallen completely?] By no means! But through their trespass salvation has come to the Gentiles, so as to make Israel jealous. [That is, when God set Israel aside, he allowed his delivering word to go out directly to Gentile peoples everywhere so that they might be the visible demonstration of how God can heal and fulfill human life, and Israel was watching—at least individual Jews have been, all along.] Now if their trespass means riches for the world, and if their failure means riches for the Gentiles, how much more will their full inclusion mean! [That is, when Israel comes back into its right relationship with God, how much more blessing will this world understand and realize when they see worked out before their eyes what a nation can be with God in its midst!] (Rom. 11:11–12).

And in Romans 11:15 Paul says, "For if their rejection means the reconciliation of the world, what will their acceptance mean but life from the dead?"

This is a dream and a vision that men have long held. Politicians have struggled for centuries to try to find the secret of world peace. Years ago I was struck by the closing words of a great address that Winston Churchill gave at Edinburgh, Scotland, in 1950:

> What prizes lie before all the people if they are worthy of them: peace, food, happiness, leisure, wealth for the

masses never known nor dreamed of, the glorious advance into a period of rest and safety for all the hundreds
of millions of homes where little children play by the
fire, and girls grow up in all their beauty, and young
men strive and win in the free enterprise of life. Around
us the storms may gather, but let us not shut out the
hope that the burdens of fear and want may be lifted
for a glorious era from the bruised and weary shoulders
of mankind.

What a beautiful dream. But is it only a dream? No.
The Lord Jesus says that he came and uncovered for a
brief time the secret of world peace and prosperity.
But he hid it again. And then he went and gave all that
he had and bought the field in which it is hidden. God
is in control. He bought the field in order that someday
he might use that treasure to cause the whole world to
blossom and to fill the earth with peace and happiness.
When the world sees again a visible manifestation of
what God intends a nation to do, then the nations will
learn world peace. They will come and study this little
nation of Israel in which the secret of world peace has
always been hidden, the strange, chosen nation for
which our Lord gave his life.

And do you know that all this is not without its
application to us as individuals as well? For Israel,
even in rejection, even in failure, is still an example to
the people of the world. If you want to see how God
will act with you as an individual, then look at the
way he has been acting with Israel as a nation. This
is why this nation is here. It is a visible example to all
mankind of the way God deals with humanity. So if
you, like Israel, have temporarily turned away from

God; if you, like Israel, have once had sweet fellowship with the Lord but lately have been resisting, have lost faith; if you are wandering in perplexity, puzzlement, and bewilderment, in obscurity, weakness, and defeat—nevertheless God's promises to you are just as sure as they are to Israel. God has said that if you will turn back to him, as Israel will some day, he stands ready to heal, ready to forgive, ready to wipe out all the failures, all the transgressions, and to begin in your experience to cause your life to blossom and come into abundance. This is God's promise to you.

Our heavenly Father, how we thank you for the marvelous truth that you, Lord, have bought the world, that it belongs to you, and that you will some day rule in power and glory in its midst, and all your promises will be fulfilled. We pray, Lord Jesus, that we may apply this to our lives and that we may understand that you desire to heal us and bring us right now into an experience of joy and glory and gladness and fruitfulness. We ask it in Jesus' name, Amen.

7

The Case
of the Valuable Pearl

The parable of the pearl of great price, as we have said, is very closely linked to the preceding parable of the buried treasure. But these two parables do not have exactly the same meaning—our Lord now desires to teach us something more:

> "Again, the kingdom of heaven is like a merchant in search of fine pearls, who, on finding one pearl of great value, went and sold all that he had and bought it" (Matt. 13:45–46).

If we will now continue to follow the suggestions which the Lord himself has given us in this series of parables, we will again have our clues to the meaning of this story. The man who is searching for the pearls is, of course, Jesus himself. He is the sower who went out to sow. He is the one who scattered the sons of the kingdom throughout the world, as he tells us. He is the one who planted the mustard seed in the field. Throughout these parables he is the one who is active in the midst of this age. So it is Jesus, then, who comes as a merchant seeking fine pearls.

This is an oriental picture; the Hebrew people never valued pearls. One of the strange things about the Old Testament is that although many jewels and gems are mentioned there—diamonds and rubies and sapphires and topazes and agates—you will find no mention of a pearl. For some reason the Hebrew people did not think highly of pearls. But Jesus' disciples were Galileans, and Galilee was a region to which many Gentile traders came looking for valuable pearls, and they would pay fabulous prices for them in order to purchase them for their kings. So the disciples understood the symbol our Lord is using here: A merchant comes seeking pearls and finds one of great value; in order to obtain it he must sell all that he has and buy it.

This parable points to the same kind of activity as we saw in the parable of the treasure hidden in the field of humanity. That treasure is the nation Israel, in which is embodied the ultimate solution to the problem of establishing world peace and harmony. Until Israel comes into a right relationship with its Messiah and Lord there is no way men can work out peaceful international relationships. To bring that nation into its own, the Lord Jesus came and gave all that he had and bought the field so that he might one day bring about world prosperity and peace. We saw that the giving of all that he had is a picture of the cross of our Lord. He gave himself. As Isaiah so beautifully expresses it, "He poured out his soul unto death" (Isa. 53:12).

ANOTHER TREASURE

But in this parable Jesus reveals another aspect of the work of the cross. We need only ask ourselves, "What other great treasure does God value in this world?" in order to discover what this pearl means. For what else has Jesus given all that he has in order to obtain? The obvious answer is *the church*. When our Lord came to this world and saw the church as God sees it, with his view of history—already complete and worth so very much, he gave all that he had so that he might obtain it. Paul must have had this very parable in mind when he wrote to the Ephesians:

> . . . Christ loved the church and gave himself up for her . . . that the church might be presented before him in splendor, without spot or wrinkle or any such thing, that she might be holy and without blemish (Eph. 5:25–27).

Why did our Lord choose the pearl to symbolize the church? Why didn't he use the ruby or the diamond or any other jewel? Simply because the pearl is the only jewel which is the product of living matter. A pearl is the response of an oyster to something which causes it injury. A pearl grows out of hurt. You probably know how a pearl is formed. A little particle of sand or some other bothersome substance gets inside the shell of the oyster and it is like cracker crumbs in bed—constantly irritating. The oyster has no way to get rid of the irritant, no means of defense except to transform the thing that is injuring it. What an apt and beautiful symbol our Lord has chosen here for the church! Just as an oyster transforms something irritating and foreign into a beautiful pearl, so our Lord, by suffering with us and for us—giving all that he had—transformed us into his Church.

IDENTIFIED WITH HEARTACHE

Nothing we have considered so far, however, can begin to exhaust the implications of that vast phrase: "he gave all that he had and bought it." I wonder if any of us at any time fully grasp the significance of that. Most of us have tried to think through the sacrifice of Jesus. We often think of it as a kind of commercial enterprise—"The Lord paid the price"—as though he were merely making a purchase in a market-place. Our terms for redemption are sometimes rather crass. Or we dwell upon the agony of the cross—its physical hurt, its anguish, the injury, the pain, the thirst, the tears, the darkness, the death. Our Lord went through all that. But we have not even remotely touched the deepest significance of the cross when we deal with it on the physical level. We won't begin to understand it until we see something of the personal emotional experience of the Lord Jesus when he entered into the human family, became one with us, and in the cross identified himself with our hurt and shame and sorrow and heartache. It is easy to sing about the wounds and the blood, the thirsting and the pain, without even beginning to touch the depth of what this phrase means. It goes far, far deeper than that. It involves the hurt in the heart of God as he fully identifies with us in all our agony and extends his forgiveness to us.

Healing human hurt is God's business. The cross is God's answer to the hurt humanity has caused. This is a hurting race we belong to. No generation has ever been more aware than this one of the hurt of human hearts. All of us hurt ourselves and we hurt each other. We do not mean to, but we do. The very efforts we make to try to satisfy ourselves and to meet our needs turn out to be damaging to others in many ways. Yet in ignorance we go right on doing the things that are hurting and destroying both ourselves and each other.

Every family, every individual bears deep and abiding scars, sometimes very evident on the surface. Most of the hurt is due to the fact that we suffer from guilt —a sense of self-condemnation and self-hate—arising out of a deep sense of failure. But this heartache is what the cross is all about. God saw the hurt in the human race. He saw the agony and misery of our struggle to try to live properly without understanding the secrets of doing so. He wanted to do something about that, but he had a problem—a problem with which every one of us is familiar.

What is your reaction when someone comes with a self-righteous air to "help" you get rid of a bad habit? From an elevated position of self-assurance, he begins to correct you, heavily implying that he can't understand how you could have allowed yourself to fall into such a state—certainly *he* would never do such a thing! Obviously, you react immediately with resentment, with the result that you don't hear a word he says. No matter how right he may be, everything he says only increases your resentment and hostility and sense of guilt. This is a mistake we parents frequently make with our children. We approach them in a spirit of condemnation and blame.

Now if self-righteousness on the part of a human being can cause us to react defensively, rendering us utterly unable to be helped, how much more does the true righteousness of God frighten us when we think of having to deal with him? As Isaiah put it, "Who among us can dwell with everlasting burnings?" (Is. 33:14). Who can stand in the presence of the holiness of God and feel the greatness of his righteous being, his spotless life and not feel condemned, wiped out? If God comes to us in his justice and righteousness, we immediately feel that we cannot stand it. That is why man has fled God, has refused to deal with him, and has tried to shove him out of his thinking. We are afraid of such a God.

HE TOOK OUR PLACE

How, then, could he reach us? In order to gain us, in order to gain the pearl which he so desperately wants and loves and cherishes, he came and gave all that he had. That means that he took our place. He came where we are. He came into the place of hurt and agony and heartache and loneliness and sorrow and shame and darkness and became what we are.

THE CASE OF THE VALUABLE PEARL   127

There is no greater commentary on this phrase than that in Paul's Second Letter to the Corinthians: "For our sake he made him to be sin who knew no sin" (2 Cor. 5:21). Sin to us is merely a label by which we gather up all the terrible wrongdoing and the aching, hurting, lonely misery of mankind. When Jesus came, without making any contribution of his own to sin ("he who knew no sin"), nevertheless, in the garden of Gethsemane and on the cross he entered fully into what we feel. He felt the hurt. He knew the aching loneliness, the heartache, the misery, the rejection— the sense of despair, of self-loathing, of emptiness and worthlessness and meaninglessness, and the awful hostility engendered by sin. He felt the condemnation of a righteous God. He entered into all of that. He gave all that he had so that when he comes to us in the midst of our hurt, he is able to say, "I know just how you feel. I've been right there. I know exactly what you are going through. I understand. I know what it has done to you, and I want to show you what I've learned through this." He can put his loving hand upon us and begin to lead us out. The writer of Hebrews says, "Although he was a Son, he learned obedience through what he suffered" (Heb. 5:8). In this way, Jesus gave all that he had so that he might heal the hurt of humanity.

Now can you see what a perfect symbol the pearl is? We are the ones who have wounded our Lord, as in that hymn we often sing:

> Died He for me, who caused His pain?
> For me who Him to death pursued?

> Amazing love! How can it be
> that Thou, my God, shouldst die for me?

That is what Jesus is telling us in this parable. He came and gave all that he had so he could take all the hurt of humanity into his own heart and know the aching agony of all that we go through. Thus he is able to touch us, heal us, and minister to us by beginning to clothe us with his own beauty. By taking of his own life, out of his wounded side, to wash away our wounds, our sins, and our guilt with his own blood, he cleanses us and imparts his life to us so that we might become more and more like him. That is what happens in an oyster. The grain of sand, the irritating substance, the cause of injury, is transmuted. The unsightly is transformed into something of beauty. And that is the action of love.

John Oxenham once wrote a little poem which catches up our Lord's attitude. It becomes our attitude as we learn how to live as Christians. He said of a friend who had injured him,

> He drew a circle that shut me out,
> Rebel, heretic, a thing to flout.
> But God and I had the wit to win:
> We drew a circle that took him in!

That is Christianity. That is what our Lord has done. He has reached out to us and is healing the hurt of our human hearts by giving all that he had.

Now let's tie these two parables together. Our Lord is showing us what he is doing in this present age which lies between his two advents. Israel, he said, is going to be hidden again in the world of humanity. Human governments will stumble on in blindness and folly, ever dreaming of world peace, but never knowing that the secret of it lies in a little nation in one obscure corner of the world. But because of that treasure our Lord bought the world so that some day the earth would be filled with righteousness as the waters cover the sea, and all the glowing, beautiful dreams of the prophets would be fulfilled.

I love to read the great passages in Isaiah and elsewhere that so magnificently describe the glory of a restored earth. In phrases of transcendent beauty, the prophets look forward to the time when the desert will blossom like the rose and the curse will be removed from nature and from the animal world. The lion will lie down with the lamb, the cow will feed with the bear, and a little child will lead them. All this is coming. Swords will be beaten into plowshares and spears into pruninghooks. Men will live in peace and harmony, each one under his own fig tree. The burdens will be lifted from the weary shoulders of mankind and the springtime of the earth will come. A beautiful passage in the Song of Solomon describes it well:

> . . . for lo, the winter is past,
>   the rain is over and gone.
> The flowers appear on the earth,
>   the time of singing has come,
> and the voice of the turtledove
>   is heard in our land (2:11–12).

INTENDED FOR THE HEAVENS

But what is the pearl to accomplish? What is it for? Notice that there is no mention of the field in connection with the pearl. It is true that the church is taken out of sorrowing humanity; it does have its purpose in this present age, as Paul tells us very plainly. Right now, the church manifests the greatness and the grace of God. But the pearl is not ultimately intended for earth. It is intended for the heavens, as we learn from Paul's letters. The pearl is lifted out of the troubled sea of human sorrow to be a people that will flash in glory upon the bosom of God for unending ages. The church will be the chief medium through which God will manifest his grace and glory in all the many ages to come.

In forming the pearl, our Lord is making for himself a glorious church without spot or wrinkle or any such thing. You and I sometimes wonder why we have to go through trouble, why we get into difficulties with each other. Even as Christians, we have a struggle getting along with one another. We have to work at it. We cannot just ignore problems that arise amongst us; they don't just disappear. We have to take the bit in our teeth and go to one another and sit down and patiently and lovingly try to work it all out.

Why do we have to go through this? Because in the process the Lord is working out all the defects in his church, healing all the hurt and the sorrow, and bringing about a glorious church—a church without spot or blemish, a glowing, translucent, beautiful pearl which will be the manifestation of the glory of God throughout unending ages.

Notice how Paul expresses this in his letter to the Ephesians:

But God, who is rich in mercy, out of the great love with which he loved us, even when we were dead through our trespasses, made us alive together with Christ (by grace you have been saved), and raised us up with him, and made us sit with him in the heavenly places in Christ Jesus, that *in the coming ages* he might show the immeasurable riches of his grace in kindness toward us in Christ Jesus. For by grace you have been saved through faith; and this is not your own doing, it is the gift of God—not because of works, lest any man should boast (Eph. 2:4–9, emphasis mine).

Our Lord has beautifully captured all this in his marvelous story of the pearl. When I was a young Christian I so much enjoyed a hymn which you hardly hear any more:

> "Holy, holy, holy,"
>   is what the angels sing,
> And I expect to help them
>   make the courts of heaven ring!
> But when we sing redemption's story,
>   they must fold their wings;
> For angels never felt the joy
>   that our salvation brings.

God is working out a vast purpose. This is a great thing to remember when you are going through times of hardship and difficulty, especially when you are going through difficult personal relationships. In the process, through the heartache and the hurt, by his marvelous ministry to us, our Lord is turning what is injurious into a translucent, glowing, beautiful pearl. As we go along, we can see layer after layer of shining nacre being added to the pearl to make it a lustrous thing of beauty, a pearl of great price which the Lord, in divine anticipation, saw when he came and for which he sold all that he had so he could purchase it for himself.

INSTRUMENTS OF GOD

God is not through with us. He is working out his purposes through the daily grind and all the turmoil and pressures and problems and perplexities of our lives. These difficulties are part of the process, so don't push them away. They are God's instruments sent to do his work in your life. Don't resist them, don't gripe and moan your way through them all. Welcome them, learn to rejoice in them, as God tells us to do. Paul exclaims, "I will . . . gladly boast of my weaknesses . . ." Why? "that the power of Christ may rest upon me" (2 Cor. 12:9). His strength is made perfect in our weakness.

As these trials come to us, God is preparing us to be an instrument for untold blessing in the coming ages throughout the far reaches of his universe so as to manifest and demonstrate the immeasurable riches of his grace. You and I have a part in that. Keep that clearly in mind, as God commands us to do when he says, "Put on the helmet of salvation," the hope of the eternal purposes of God which will keep your mind straight and hold you steady in the midst of the pressures and varying uncertainties of this present hour. As Paul says, ". . . this slight momentary affliction is preparing for us an eternal weight of glory beyond all comparison" (2 Cor. 4:17).

Now, the world knows nothing of this glory. You will never see it heralded in the pages of your newspaper nor in some magazine like *Time* or *Newsweek*. The world does not understand God's purposes. But God sees history differently than we. We see a long record of civilizations and kingdoms and battles, and of explorations and discoveries. But those are only the merest incidentals. God looks at history and sees the human hurt and heartache and pain and anguish. He sees the healing of love and the understanding of grace. And he sees a new thing being formed—the pearl of great price. No wonder someone has called this earth of ours "God's Treasure Island." Hidden in it is the treasure of the field which will bring to pass at last the hopes and the dreams of men for world peace. And hidden also is this marvelous mystery of the pearl which will at last accomplish God's purposes in planets and stars and solar systems far beyond our own in that great day when God brings about all that he has planned.

We thank you, our heavenly Father, that your love and grace has planned and provided for us throughout all the eternal future. Thank you for lifting our eyes above the mediocre, above the daily routine of our lives, above all the hurt and the anguish of our days, and for helping us to see that a great and mighty purpose is being worked out. Thank you, Father, that we have a part in it, that our lives have meaning, that we move to an appointed end, that you are accomplishing your work through the things that we experience. Thank you for that healing of love and grace which transmutes and transfigures beauty. Help us not to reject your ministry to us but to accept it and to give thanks for it. We ask in Jesus' name, Amen.

8

The Case
of the Great Dragnet

Jesus told these seven parables to convey what he calls "the secrets of the kingdom of heaven." The implications of each small illustration are so vast that in examining them as closely as we have, we are likely to lose sight of the continuity that is built into the whole series by our Lord. I would like to take a brief space here to string them all together in order to restore our perspective. As we look back over this series, we can see through the eyes of our Lord something of what has been happening in our present age. We can see the history of this age as God sees it and understand something of what he is accomplishing through it. Since we are still involved in it, it has great meaning for us.

Jesus told us that the age would be characterized by

135

a sowing of truth. There would be a spreading of the ultimate message of reality, which is exactly what the gospel is. The good news is that God is telling men what the lost secret of their humanity is. The gospel is a declaration to human hearts that the cause of all their misery is that they are not operating according to the provision nor on the program which God intended for man in the beginning. That provision is God himself, living within man, invited into our lives by faith, received as Savior and Lord. The good news is that God has found a way, despite our rejection, to bring us that message again and to open up our eyes to see and understand it. That message has been sown throughout the world, as our Lord made clear in the first parable. Some would receive it—not everyone, but some—and those who would receive it would begin to grow and develop and blossom into the kind of men and women that God had in mind in the beginning.

Then in the second parable Jesus told us that there would be a scattering throughout the whole earth of the people who had responded to the truth of the gospel. The Lord said he would be responsible to place his people throughout the whole structure of humanity, geographically and socially—in every tribe and nation around the world and in every class of society.

A few years ago I attended a conference in the mountains of southern California with a group from a church made up largely of middle-class American citizens. But into this group rode a young man and his wife on motorcycles. They were dressed in black jackets with emblems emblazoned on the backs and both had long hair. They looked for all the world like Hell's Angels. I found out that indeed they had been Hell's Angels and that they are still living and traveling and working with them. But these two have become Christians and now their whole ministry is to the Hell's Angels. They perform it at great risk to themselves. They told me that after they had become Christians the other members of the gang gathered around and said, "Look, we don't mind your getting religion. We don't even mind your talking to us about it. But you'd better never be phony about it. If we ever sense that you're putting us on, we'll kill you!" Now that is quite a challenge—to minister under those terms. But that is testimony to the Lord's ability to sow his people wherever he wants them to be. This is what has been happening throughout history.

In that same parable Jesus said that another sowing would be going on conducted by the devil. He too would have his people everywhere, penetrating every class of society, and especially invading the church so that the good and the evil would grow up together until the harvest. These words of our Lord have certainly been worked out in history.

In the third parable we saw the growth of the mustard seed which our Lord planted, the little seed with its pungent, biting quality which, again, represents the gospel, with its power to stimulate and change and transform people. And yet, in a strange and unnatural way, the seed grew up into a huge,

ungainly tree with many branches in which evil birds
nest. This, too, has proven true in history as we have
seen the humble, lowly seed of the gospel by the
strange twist of counterfeit Christianity grow into a
proud and prominent church which seeks after prestige
and favor and position and power among men. This
condition is still prevalent throughout Christendom in
both Catholic and Protestant branches and is still
producing much of the untoward reaction against
genuine Christianity which we find on every side today.

The fourth parable is of the woman who hid leaven
in three measures of meal. By this Jesus indicated that
some of those in authority in the church, who should
have known better, would stray from studying and
teaching the Word of God. Neglectfully in some cases,
and deliberately in others, they would allow various
forms of sin and evil to enter into the life of the church.
This would corrupt and disrupt the precious fellowship of God's people with him and with each other.
And we know that all too often, not only today but all
through history as well, this has been the case. Im-
pediments to a consistent walk with the Lord have
been erected, and disharmony, discord, and turmoil
have arisen between individuals and groups and fac-
tions of genuine believers just as Jesus warned.

Then there were the two parables of the treasure
hidden in the field and of the valuable pearl, which,
taken together, give us the purpose of the cross—the
reason Jesus died. He came and gave all that he had
in order to purchase the field of humanity which contains the treasure of the secret of world peace and

prosperity. And that secret, we saw, is bound up in a tiny nation, Israel, which has been brought back into being in very recent times. It is now very much in the forefront of human events, occupying the center of the stage in current history, as the world is only now becoming dimly aware. All this is happening because God has a purpose for that nation. And when he teaches them again the secret of their own lives, there will come that time of world peace and prosperity of which the prophets have spoken.

Jesus also gave all that he had in order to purchase the valuable pearl of a redeemed humanity, to impart to individuals the secret of peace and of meaning in life and thus to fashion a new community—a whole new race of people who would have a wonderful purpose far beyond this life and beyond this planet in God's great program for the ages. This is the pearl of great price, which is the church.

That brings us to the parable of the great dragnet. These are Jesus' words:

> "Again, the kingdom of heaven is like a net which was thrown into the sea and gathered fish of every kind; when it was full, men drew it ashore and sat down and sorted the good into vessels but threw away the bad. So it will be at the close of the age. The angels will come out and separate the evil from the righteous, and throw them into the furnace of fire; there men will weep and gnash their teeth" (Matt. 13:47–50).

FORCED INTO THE OPEN

The television serial Dragnet (remember: dum, da dum dum?) captured the intent of this parable better than any commentary I have in my library. It was

about a police dragnet which swept through the city
of Los Angeles to capture and bring in all kinds of
people to be investigated so that either their badness
or goodness in the eyes of the law might be exposed.
Incidentally, it was even located in the right place,
the City of the Angels, because in this parable our
Lord associates angels with the judgment.

That program was an apt description of what is going on in our present day. There is a characteristic of
the gospel which forces individuals out into the open
where they can be seen for what they really are. There
is an element in this radical message of Christianity
which exposes people when they come into contact
with it. It makes known what they are, just as a great
dragnet sweeping through the seas gathering fish of
every kind ultimately exposes whether they are good or
bad, as our Lord makes clear. This has been happening
throughout our age. The radical truth of the gospel
is like a net seining through the tides of restless, surg-
ing humanity, and whoever is caught in it is forced to
declare himself, forced out into the open to reveal
whether he is bad or good.

Now, do not misunderstand me; people are not
simply born bad or good. We are all part of a fallen
race. We are all born into lost humanity. We all have
evil at work within us, and that evil will create in our
character a resistance to truth if God does not intervene. We are all in that condition. Bad or good, in this
parable, refers to how we respond to truth and what
happens when we come into contact with reality. That
is the whole issue. The gospel of Jesus Christ is the

basic truth, the ultimate reality, the fundamental secret of life, the way things really are. The good are
those who deal honestly with this reality, who respond
to it, act on it, do something about it. The bad are
those who, at best, turn their backs on the gospel and
deliberately reject it, and at worst, play the hypocrite
—accepting the gospel in appearance only, but not
allowing it to make any changes in their lives. These
remain essentially evil within although they are outwardly pious.

Life presents many illusions. We do not always perceive difference between truth and falsehood. All of
us, even the youngest among us, have learned that you
cannot trust everything you see. Many ideas are pro-
pounded today as being delightful and capable of
bringing you happiness. But when you grasp them,
they are like cobwebs, melting to dust in your hands,
and you are left frustrated, disillusioned and disappointed, or shattered and defeated. Life consists of
trying to sort out the illusions from the truth, of at-
tempting to distinguish between fantasy and the real
thing.

The truth is that man was created to be indwelt by
God. The only way we can fulfill our humanity is to
be filled with God and to understand that we are to
live, to operate, by faith in him. The gospel message,
this good news about the lost secret of humanity, about
the fact that Christ in you is able to restore to you all
that God ever intended you to have, is like a great net
sweeping through the tides of humanity. Whoever is
caught in it is made to reveal what kind of people they

are, to reveal whether they will deal honestly with the truth or whether they will reject it and turn from it. You can see this process in your own life, in your own experience. You can see it in the record of church history. You can see this radical character of the gospel working itself out in human events today.

WHEN YOU HEAR THE TRUTH

When Paul spoke to the Athenians on Mars Hill, to the thinkers and philosophers in that great pagan city where the people were given over to superstition and to the worship of false gods, he said to them,

> The times of ignorance [the foolish worshiping of false ideas and following after false gods] God overlooked [he ignored it because he does not ever condemn people for ignorance], but now he commands all men everywhere to repent, because he has fixed a day on which he will judge the world in righteousness by a man [Jesus] whom he has appointed, and of this he has given assurance to all men by raising him from the dead (Acts 17:30–31).

What did he mean by that? Paul's phrase, "but now," does not refer to a moment in history before which men were allowed to live in ignorance but from which time on they all have to believe. He is referring to a point in the experience of each individual. We are all born into ignorance. We all grow up following false gods, committed to wrong ideals, and operating on false principles. But when you hear the truth of the gospel, when the reality of Jesus Christ risen from the dead strikes you and you understand that in the resurrection of Jesus God has demonstrated before all the world the availability of a wholly different way of life, that there is a new provision for man, and that in Jesus Christ is found the lost secret of our humanity— when you learn that—then you have arrived at a crisis point, then you have to do something about it. You have to act on it or reject it, one or the other.

From then on you will be different. The truth will drive you one way or the other. If you believe it and act upon it, you will never be the same again. It will change everything about your life, gradually, little by little, as you see it applied to various areas. If you reject it, you will never be the same again. You will either be constantly playing the hypocrite, becoming more pious outwardly and more devilish inwardly, or you will turn your back on Christianity altogether and go your own way to become a blatantly atheistic philosopher, spreading propaganda against God everywhere you go. That is what Jesus is saying. His dragnet exposes the attitude of your heart toward the truth.

You can see that in this passage from Paul's Second Letter to the Corinthians, where he says,

> But thanks be to God, who in Christ always leads us in triumph, and through us spreads the fragrance of the knowledge of him everywhere. For we are the aroma of Christ to God among those who are being saved and among those who are perishing, to one a fragrance from death to death, to the other a fragrance from life to life (2 Cor. 2:14–16).

Everywhere Paul went he made an impact and an impression, and people could never be the same because when they understood the great, thrusting reality of the gospel, they had to make a choice. What they determined to do exposed whether they were honest or not, whether they wanted to deal with life as it is or to fool themselves and go on dreaming about something that would never be. Christians are the aroma of Christ to all men. Wherever we go, men must face a fact which changes them. And they go on either from life to life, growing in grace and freedom and liberty, or from death to death, ending in the death of eternal loss.

Our Lord foresaw that this would occur throughout the age. But at the close of the age, he says, there will be a public manifestation of this division among men. In other words, throughout the age, now almost twenty centuries long, the division has been taking place in the lives of individuals. Anybody hearing this message has been revealed in the eyes of God to be either bad or good, unrealistic or honest. But as the age draws to a close the time will come when this division between men, this frank declaration of where people actually are, will come clearly into the open. Our Lord says, "So it will be at the close of the age. The angels will come out and separate the evil from the righteous. . . ."

It is very important that we understand what Jesus means when he uses the term, "the close of the age." He is talking about a period of time which the prophets had specified would close the age of the Gentiles. Daniel said it would be seven years long and that during that time strange events would occur in human affairs. Jesus himself describes it in the twenty-fourth chapter of the Book of Matthew. He tells us that the close of the age will be recognizable because it will be a time of "great tribulation, such as has not been from the beginning of the world until now, no, and never will be" (Matt. 24:21). There have been some terrible times in the past, but nothing men have experienced will measure up to this time of judgment. It is during the last seven years of this present age, before our Lord returns in power and glory with all his angels, as he himself describes, that this judgment takes place and the angels separate the good from the bad.

ACCOMPLISHED BY ANGELS

Now, Jesus said that this separation would be accomplished by the angels, not by men. On the basis of the Word of God I believe in angels. I have never seen one, but I believe in them. The Bible teaches that angels are ministering spirits sent forth to minister to those who will be the heirs of salvation (Heb. 1:14). I believe in recording angels who keep a record of what we are doing. I don't know how they do it, but I believe they do. I believe in guardian angels who protect us from serious disaster. I know I keep mine busy most of the time.

There have been several times in history, including the time our Lord was here on earth, when angels have been visibly present among men and manifest in their activity. When the disciples went to the tomb, they found angels guarding it and explaining the events of the resurrection. When Jesus ascended into the heavens, two angels robed in white stood by to explain to the disciples what had happened. As we approach the close of the age, it may well be that this kind of angelic visitation will be evident once again. I don't know how it will be received by people. Since it will be apparent that angels are a different sort of being from ourselves, their presence on earth is apt to be explained as some kind of invasion from outer space.

Whatever men may think of them, Jesus says that at the close of the age the angels will be active. Angels have never ceased to be active, but for the most part their activity has been behind the scenes. Wherever angels are at work, there is invisible, divine activity with visible and yet otherwise unexplainable results. Something often happens in human affairs which cannot be explained by the people who make it their business to study and analyze trends in human reactions and thoughts. They can only record it, but do not know why it is happening. Most likely, however, it is a manifestation of some kind of angelic activity.

The dividing work of the angels, as we saw in the parable of the wheat and tares, has already begun. Jesus said the angels would be working to drive evil and good into separate clusters of men and women. In this parable the division is fully effected, and what every man is will be known to all.

In other words, as we draw near to the end of the age, hypocrisy is going to be more and more difficult. It will be harder to pretend to be a Christian. More and more people will be driven into an open manifestation of the evil that is within and will no longer be able to cloak it with some form of outward righteousness. That will be the result of angelic activity, exposing the bad in order that it might be destroyed and allowing the good to remain for the harvest of God, as this parable makes very clear.

I am not at all certain how this final division is going to work out in history; our Lord does not give us the details. But I am sure this trend will occur; in fact, it may well be occurring right now. The issues are becoming increasingly clear, and it is not as easy as it used to be to hide behind a facade of counterfeit Christianity. The reality must be there. The whole trend in our day toward honesty, this cry of a whole generation for reality and genuineness, is probably the result of the activity of angels moving us toward this final manifestation.

JESUS AND JUDGMENT

Notice that our Lord closes with a very solemn word: "The angels will come out and separate the evil from the righteous, and throw them into the furnace of fire; there men will weep and gnash their teeth." Weeping speaks of remorse and sorrow. Gnashing of teeth speaks of frustration and hostility and anger. It is all gathered up in the burning phrase, "the furnace of fire." I do not know fully what that means. And I do not like judgment any more than you do. I have always been uneasy whenever I have had to deal with these passages which speak of hell and judgment, of death and of the wrath of God. I don't like to think that God will have to appear in blazing judgment one of these days. But I have been helped greatly by recognizing that in the New Testament the one who speaks most often and most solemnly about judgment and wrath and flames is Jesus himself. The One with the outstretched arms, with the compassionate heart, who longs to heal sick and wounded humanity, is the One who speaks also about the ultimate end of those who turn their backs and refuse the healing grace of God. So we must live with this passage the way it is. Our Lord is simply indicating that the issue sharpens as we draw to the close of the age and that at the end it will no longer be possible to hide. As he himself said in another connection, ". . . nothing is covered that will not be revealed . . . and what you hear whispered, proclaim upon the housetops" (Matt. 10: 26–27). That which has been hidden in obscurity and which we think we have gotten away with will be exposed before the gaze of all.

HOW DOES YOUR LOVE GROW?

The final question which this parable leaves with us is this: Are you really changed by your contact with Jesus Christ and are you still changing? Everyone, in one way or another, has had a contact, a touch, with Jesus, has heard his voice. What has it done to you? What has happened? Are you gradually moving more and more into wholesomeness, into health of spirit, into a departure from childish ideas and actions? Are you becoming genuine and loving and concerned for others? Or does your form of Christianity leave you unchanged within, outwardly pious and respectable—outwardly part of the Christian community, singing the hymns, attending the meetings, doing all the expected things, but inwardly just as bitter and resentful, just as self-centered and concerned for your own ends, seeking after prestige and favor and advancement just as much as you always have been, only perhaps more difficult to live with at home? That is what this parable is driving at.

When we are dealing with God, we are not dealing with someone who can be bought off. We are dealing with ultimate reality, striking deep into our lives and exposing whatever it finds. And the only way we can meet this reality with any possibility of survival and chance of acceptance is with honesty, simple honesty —just saying what we are. When we do, the healing glory of Jesus Christ is able to take us and remove the evil from our hearts and restore the good, to change us into the kind of people we want to be and God wants us to be. As we come to the close of this searching parable we need to pray David's great prayer:

> Search me, O God, and know my heart!
>   Try me and know my thoughts!
> And see if there be any wicked way in me,
>   and lead me in the way everlasting! (Ps. 139:23–24).

That is the only ground upon which ultimately we can stand before our Lord. The final, ultimate test is a searching one. Our Lord describes it again in Matthew 25 in his story of the separation of the sheep from the goats when he comes again. The test is, "As you did it to one of the least of these my brethren, you did it to me" (Matt. 25:40). Inasmuch as your inward motivation, your whole heart, has been awakened with compassion for those who are hungry and sick and in prison, then you have been changed. But if your brand of Christianity is only that of mere outward form, of respectability, a certain moral standard, a degree of a "live and let live" attitude, and yet you have no compassion, no willingness to reach out and expend yourself to meet the need of someone else, then you have never been changed. God has yet to do a work of grace in your heart. This is where this parable leaves us.

As we bring this study to a close, we can see how our Lord has clearly and completely captured all the great trends of our day and our age. He brings us at last now to stand naked and open before him, and all that we are is made clear. Our only hope is to say, "Lord, here I am. I cannot change myself. I can only admit what I am and put myself in your hands. And you, Lord, can change me."

We ask you now, Lord Jesus, to measure each heart and show each of us what our own heart is. May there be many who will pray, "Lord Jesus, change me. I am just what I am, and I cannot change myself. But I do not want to be what I am any longer. Lord, please change me." Many of us are Christians already, Lord, and we really have believed in you. But there are areas of our lives in which we are still resisting you, still trying to pretend that we are something we are not. So we ask you, Lord Jesus, to change those areas too, to redeem them. Help us to acknowledge them and claim your healing grace. We ask in your name, Amen.

9

Trained for the Kingdom

We have already studied the last of these parables of the kingdom so perhaps you thought we were through with this passage. But Jesus added a very revealing postscript, or epilogue, which is of extreme importance. Without it our understanding of this great passage would be incomplete. Let's begin with our Lord's words in verse 51. He asks his disciples,

"Have you understood all this?" They said to him, "Yes." And he said to them, "Therefore every scribe who has been trained for the kingdom of heaven is like a householder who brings out of his treasure what is new and what is old" (Matt. 13:51, 52).

Jesus prefaces this most remarkable statement with a question: "Have you understood this?" We are almost startled by the disciples' answer; very naively and in-

genuously they simply reply, "Yes." Without any
questions, without a word of explanation, without a
single reservation on their part they say, "Yes, we
have understood you." Our Lord goes on, then, to
show them something very remarkable about themselves. And since we also are related to him as disciples, just as they were, what he says applies to us as
well.

YOU ARE SCRIBES

The Lord uses a seemingly incongruous term to
describe his disciples at this point. He says, "Therefore," that is, because you say you understand this,
"every scribe who has been trained for the kingdom of
heaven is like a householder . . ." He says his disciples are *scribes*. That is startling, because the scribes
were enemies of Jesus! As the gospel accounts reveal,
there were three classes of people who opposed our
Lord's ministry and who were constantly throwing ob-
stacles in his path. There were the chief priests, and
the rulers (members of the Sanhedrin, the ruling
council), and the scribes. These three groups continually tried to trap Jesus in his own words in order to
get him into trouble with the Roman authorities. The
scribes were particularly persistent in coming to him
with questions designed to trick him. They were the
ones who constantly tried to stir up the people against
him. Yet when our Lord comes to the close of this
message he says to his disciples, "You are *scribes* who
have been trained for the kingdom of heaven."

We need to reach back into the Old Testament

books of Ezra and Nehemiah to find out who the scribes were in history. Ezra was the first of the scribes. He was a leader among the remnant of the Jews who returned to Jerusalem from Babylon after the Captivity. The first arrivals had found the city of Jerusalem in utter ruins; the temple was completely destroyed. The Jews were authorized to rebuild the temple and the city and especially to restore the worship of God in the temple. But first, the spirit of the people had to be built up. To do that Ezra took the Law of Moses and began to teach the people out of the Law. Chapter 8 of Nehemiah records that a pulpit of wood was built for Ezra. (This, by the way, is the first time a pulpit appears in Scripture.) Standing upon it he began to speak to them from the Scriptures, to interpret the Law of Moses, explaining what it meant.

That was the beginning of the ministry of the scribes. At first it was a very helpful ministry. But men soon came in who carried on the form of this ministry but whose words were rigid and narrow and whose interpretive opinions were unsupported by the Scriptures. Thus the scribes, who began as authoritative interpreters of the Law, became a group of legalistic, self-righteous teachers, as our Lord found them in his day.

Nevertheless, Jesus uses this very word and says, "You disciples are scribes. You are to be authoritative interpreters of the word of God. You are like men trained in the kingdom of heaven." In other words, the disciples of Jesus Christ, including all believers everywhere, are men and women who are being taught how God works in the affairs of men. We are learning, gradually, the secrets of the divine activity behind the scenes of history, and behind the personal events in our own lives. That is what a scribe is for. He is to understand, to be trained, and to be discipled in the secrets of the kingdom of heaven.

How desperately such scribes are needed today! I observe people getting into all manner of arguments because they do not understand what God is doing. But it is the business of Christians to understand life. That is what Jesus is saying to his disciples. These are people who are being trained for the kingdom of heaven, which means they are being trained to see what God is doing. The kingdom of heaven is God at work in the affairs of men, and the disciples are being told how to perceive what he is doing and understand it. It is the business of Christians to learn how to live realistically and with increasing success. We are to learn how to cope with life and handle its problems through an increasing understanding of God's processes at work in our lives.

THE WORLD IS WATCHING

I like to stress this because I find so many people who think becoming a Christian is just a way to get to heaven when you die. Thank God, it does include going to heaven. That is kind of a fringe benefit you receive as a Christian, and there *is* a great future ahead for believers. But that is not why God has called you *now* to be a Christian. Or, to put it another way, that is not why he has left you here. He has left you to learn how to live. We are given the same sort of struggles and problems common to men and women who are not Christians, but our task is to learn how to solve them. When non-Christians look at our lives they ought to be able to see the problems increasingly being solved. That is what gives them the confidence to believe that the message we preach is a genuine message, a message of reality and truth.

If, on the other hand, as has been happening so much in the last decade, non-Christians looking at Christians see nothing but the same miserable set of problems that they themselves are struggling with, but unsolved, they have a right to wonder what difference Christianity makes. If they see Christian homes torn with strife and bickering, quarreling and fighting, if they see marriages split right down the middle and Christians getting divorces, if they see sexual immorality prevailing in Christian lives as much as in non-Christian, then they are quite justified to ask us, "What is your message for? What does it do? Why should we be interested? You're not doing any better than we are."

That is why the Scriptures always stress that Christianity consists of far more than merely believing a set of doctrines or creeds; it is demonstrating a life. Anything short of that is an abortive and distorted picture of Christian life, and the world is constantly watching. What Jesus is teaching his disciples here at the close of this great message is that this transformation of life is not a single act of magic. It is not accomplished immediately upon the conversion of an individual. It begins there, but that is only the beginning. It is not accomplished, for example, by going forward at a Billy Graham Crusade and receiving Jesus Christ as your Lord and Savior. That is the way to begin, and your life will undoubtedly show an immediate change for the better in some ways. You will indeed experience a kind of peace and forgiveness that you have never known before, which is a real cause for rejoicing and thanksgiving. But that is not the end; it is just the beginning!

This is what so few Christians seem to understand. When you become a Christian, you are introduced into a continual transforming process which ought to exhibit increasingly the healing and the wholeness of life. We are all in that process. Nobody ever arrives at the end of it in this life. But it ought to be evident that visible and continual progress is being made.

When the Lord speaks to his disciples after revealing to them the secrets of the kingdom of heaven, the question he asks them is very important because it marks the beginning of that process. He asks them, "Do you understand what I've been saying?" Obviously, this is the place to begin. How can we hope to know what life is *all* about unless we understand *something* about it?

Every one of us has experienced the fact that life is filled with much confusion and delusion. Many times we cannot distinguish what is true from what is false. We are offered many things which we consider to be filled with promise, and we hope they will do something for us. The world around us is constantly urging us to try them, telling us that we will be denying ourselves if we don't. So we try them and discover that the promises are empty. They do not deliver. We have grasped cobwebs. Life is a continual process of trying things which seem to offer success and help only to find out that they are absolutely phony promises. And so we end up disenchanted and disillusioned with life.

What we need, obviously, is understanding. We need a way to find out about these things without having to try every one of them. We need a way to know the difference between the true and the false, the phony and the real, without investing most of our lives in the process. That is exactly what our Lord came to give us. In his First Letter John says, "And we know that the Son of God has come and has given us understanding . . ." (1 John 5:20). That is the great theme of the good news of the gospel! It is a faithful revelation to us of the way things really are. God has set life up on the foundation of the truth as it is in Jesus. And it is going to be that way whether we accept it or reject it, whether we like it or not. Those facts are going to stand unshakeable. That is what Jesus meant when he said, "Heaven and earth shall pass away, but my word shall never pass away." Why? Because his word is fact, it is utter reality.

You know how facts are. You can attack them and ignore them and skirt around them and try to forget them. But when you get all through, there they are— staring you right in the face. No matter how you have tried to deceive yourself about them, you cannot get by with it forever. Ultimately, you must turn around, after going down many and many a blind alley, and come back and look the facts squarely in the face and agree, "Yes, that is the way things are. I can't change it." That is what Jesus has come to tell us. That is what the Word of God is all about. It is the revelation of things the way they really are. To me the glory of being a Christian is that I do not have to go through all the agonizing pain of trying out everything that comes along. I can find out about it by the Word.

UNDERSTANDING THE DEFINITIONS

That is why Jesus says, "Do you understand these things?" That is where it begins. There must be a clear understanding that what God is saying is true and that you know what he means. And the disciples answer very naively, "Yes." I don't think they were being dishonest. They were just like we are. They meant that they had an intellectual apprehension of the words that he used. They knew the meaning of the symbols he employed. So they said, as perhaps you are now saying after studying through these parables with me, "Yes, we understand them. We know what you meant. We know that when you were talking about the pearl of great price, you were referring to the church. When you were talking about the hidden treasure, you meant the nation Israel. We know that the mustard seed represents the whole enterprise of Christendom in the world today, growing into power and splendor and prestige among men. Yes, we understand these things."

But as you watch these disciples, they reveal that they do not *understand* what he meant. Their actions soon show that they have only a very limited and shallow understanding of what he was talking about, just as we do. We can easily identify with them. Suppose somebody asked you, "Do you understand beauty?" How foolish you would be to say, "Yes." Who understands beauty or love or death or life? These are but words. We may understand the definitions of the words, but who really understands the subjects? None of us.

These disciples remind me of the boy who was not paying much attention in his physics class. Noticing this, his professor suddenly asked him a question: "Jack, will you tell me what electricity is?" The boy, caught unaware, did not even hear the question. But trying to seem sharp, he said, "Well, sir, I'm sorry. I had the answer on the tip of my tongue just a moment ago but it has escaped me right now." And the professor said, "What a pity. What a pity! The only man in the history of the world who has ever known what electricity is, and he's forgotten it already!" That is the position the disciples are in.

But Jesus goes on to show them that a deeper process is necessary for real understanding. He says that this process consists of two elements. Everyone who is being trained in the kingdom of heaven, man or woman, boy or girl, whoever is learning to recognize how God works in human life, is going to have to go through this process. He will be like a householder, a home owner, who takes new and old things out of his treasury. That sounds very much like the description of a garage sale, but that is not what our Lord has in mind. The householder is the head of the house. He is an authoritative figure. Jesus is the only one in the Scriptures who ever uses this term for a householder. In Greek the word is *oikodespotes*—house-despot, house director. He says that every disciple who is learning the process of life is like a man who is the head of a home and who is constantly taking out of his resources two kinds of things—new things and old things—and putting them together.

WHAT'S NEW?

What are these new and old things? Well, since Jesus is talking about life, as he always does, you can see immediately what they are. The things that are new are the constantly changing experiences of our lives. Every one of us comes each day into new and fresh experiences. Right now I am experiencing certain things that I have never experienced before because I have never before been the age I am now.

And you are running into new experiences. Perhaps you are starting out right now with the experience of marriage. You have never had that relationship before; it is brand new. Or you are beginning parenthood. You have never had a child before, and no matter how many millions have gone through it before you, it is all fresh and new to you. If you are recent graduates of school, you are starting out in a new relationship with the world which you have never had before. Life is made up of new things.

Ah, yes, but there are also old things. The old things are the abiding things, the eternal, unalterable principles, the unchanging relationships which never have varied for all of human time but remain the same forever. There are things like that. The nature of God is one. Human nature never changes either. Basic family relationships—fathers with children, brothers with sisters—never change. There are issues that never change. Evil and good remain the same. Laws of morality and physics never change; they abide forever.

Perhaps you have heard the story of a man who went to see an old music teacher who was a friend of his. When he knocked on the door, his old friend greeted him. And the man, in the flippant way we moderns often do, said, "Hi! What's the good news for today?" The old music teacher didn't say a word. He just went back into the room, picked up a little rubber hammer, and struck a tuning fork that was hanging there. As the note sounded throughout the room, he said, "That is 'A'. Now, that was 'A' five thousand years ago and that will be 'A' five thousand years in the future. The soprano across the hall sings off-key. The piano downstairs is out of tune. The baritone upstairs flats his high notes. But," he said, striking the tuning fork again, "that is 'A', and that, my friend, is the good news for today!"

And that is true, isn't it? There are fundamental things which have never changed. One of the satanic lies that is being foisted upon our searching, deeply-feeling generation is that there is nothing which remains unchanged, that everything is relative. That is a lie! There are great things which never have changed and never will change. As long as the universe is here, and even beyond that time, as long as God exists, there are things that never will change—things old. And the business of life, the process which will make you an authoritative interpreter of life so that people will listen to your words and heed what you say, is constantly to discover how to take the things old and the things new—the changing experiences of your life and the unchanging, eternal truth of God—and bring them together.

PUTTING THEM TOGETHER

Life itself will teach you some of the old things. You do not need a Bible to discover some of them. But the great place where the revelation of things old is found is in the Word of God. There you can learn what is real and what you can count on, what will not disappear or fold under you when you put your weight upon it. The business of life is to understand these things. Jesus is saying that you can start with an intellectual grasp of them, but you will never understand them until you put the two together—things new and things old. Then you will understand life. Then you will be trained for the kingdom of heaven.

You know how this can happen. Perhaps the order may vary. Sometimes it is the new which illustrates and explains the old. Sometimes, right in the middle of some kind of experience or after we have emerged from it, we suddenly realize that a passage of Scripture is being illuminated so that for the first time we understand what the old has said. It has come alive to us. And we never forget that lesson. We may have read that passage repeatedly for years, but it didn't seem to say anything much to us until our experience, the new thing, explained the old thing.

Our family has been discussing certain family needs, including the needs of children to be loved and accepted and given a sense of self-appreciation, a sense of their own value. These must be supplied by parents. Children are designed to learn from their parents the need for responding to love and the need for evaluating their lives and seeing themselves as persons of worth who have a place in God's program. It is the parents' task to make this known to their children, to help them to see themselves as appreciated and loved. This kind of relationship between parents and children is designed to lead the children on to God, so they come to know and trust him as an unseen Father because they have come to know and trust the father they see.

As we were discussing this, someone asked, "Well, what if this doesn't happen? What if fathers and mothers don't show this kind of love? Or what if an accident occurs and they are gone and the child is left homeless, an orphan, and no one is there to teach him; then what? Can he learn it directly from God?" And immediately there came flashing into my mind a verse from Psalm 27: "When my father and my mother forsake me, then the Lord will take me up." I understood something about that which I have never understood before. God does not intend to teach children about himself directly when they have fathers and mothers who can teach them about him. His business is to work out this relationship with the fathers and mothers so that the children can learn through them. It is unlikely that a child will really learn how to trust and love God as long as his parents are there and could teach him about God but are not doing so. This passage came clear to me, then, and along with it all the great promises of his concern which God gives throughout the Old Testament. He promises to be a father to the fatherless, a husband to the widow, and to meet such needs where there is no human person to do so.

TURN TO THE OLD

But more often it is the old which unveils and unravels the new. You encounter an experience in which you don't know what to do. You are under pressure, being torn, and everything is going wrong, so you begin to ask, "What's wrong? What should I do?" That is the time to turn to the old, to let the old explain the new, to apply to life the great principles and teachings of the Scriptures and, as the old begins to unravel the new, that problem will begin to be solved.

As a pastor, I have seen this work so frequently. So many times I have heard someone say, "I don't know what's wrong with my marriage!" But then, as the husband learns from the Scriptures that a husband's role is to give himself to his wife, to communicate with her, to talk to her, to open up his life and let her in, to let her see what his needs and responses are, to share with her, the marriage begins to heal. That is because the principles undergirding the relationship of marriage are fundamental and unchanging.

Or I have seen the wife begin to understand from the Scriptures that her role is to stop trying to manipulate and maneuver behind the scenes, to stop forcing her husband to do things by means of those subtle, quiet little ways which husbands call nagging. She is to begin to trust her husband—not in everything, that cannot be done at first—but in some things, and in little ways she is to begin to trust her husband's leadership and follow him. And suddenly she discovers that the marriage begins to heal. Why? Because the old has solved the problem of the new.

This happens in quarrels. Jesus' fundamental law for handling quarrels between human beings is that you must begin with yourself. "First, *first,* remove the beam that is in your own eye, *then* you will see clearly how to help your brother." Yet we always try to turn it around, don't we? We want *them* to change. "If they'll do this, then I'll do that." But it will never work on that basis, *never.* For all eternity, if you try to work out a difficult relationship on that basis, it will never work. But let the old reveal the new, and things begin to work out.

Fears: How many people are afraid today! The answer to fear is faith. But it begins small, in little ventures, not in big, sudden leaps into an unknown future. Rather, the building of faith begins in little testings of the reality of God, trying him out and seeing that he can be depended upon, and then moving on further.

Gradually fear begins to fade as faith takes over, and love is born, for perfect love casts out fear.

That is what Christianity is all about. It is a life-healing process. It is designed to change us and make us whole. Apart from visible evidence of that wholeness, we have nothing to say to the world around. They must see this healing taking place in our midst. Jesus says that you can never speak with authority, you can never be a scribe, interpreting the law, merely by having a "head knowledge" of the doctrine of Scripture. Authority will come only as you have undergone the process of taking things old and things new and putting them together. Out of that experience you can say, "Let me share with you a lesson God has taught me. I got the clue from the Word; I began to apply it to my situation, and this is what happened. God has healed, and I want to share this with you." That is the kind of Christianity to which the world listens and responds.

> Our heavenly Father, we ask you to teach us from your Word in such a way that we gain not only a mental understanding of the doctrine but the actual manifestation of it in practice in our lives. Heal us, Lord, by your marvelous, powerful Word which will always accomplish that purpose for which you have sent it. Help us to take these great things that are old and put them together rightly with the things that are new, and thus learn how to be true scribes in the kingdom of heaven. We ask in your name, Amen.